*It is my ...rd*

Job 23:10
Psalm (2)
Philippians 4:13
Romans 8:28
1st John 1:9

*Some degree of help, hope, comfort, faithfulness, and encouragement within these pages.*

# I Walked
## the Darkest Valleys
## to Freedom

*By David Harold Pedersen*
*BS, MS, CCC-A.A.A.*

RoseDog Books
PITTSBURGH, PENNSYLVANIA 15238

Rosedog Publishing Co
585 Alpha Drive
Pittsburgh, PA 15238

Visit our website at www.rosedogbookstore.com

ISBN: 978-1-64957-939-3
eISBN: 978-1-64957-960-7

Dedicated to the loving memory of my parents,
little sister Coreen, Sheila's twin, and other family members
who have left this world too soon.

In my anguish I cried to the Lord,
and he answered by setting me free.
Psalm 118:5

# FOREWORD

Very few books contain a riveting, active, melancholy story of life that is about feelings from a heart filled with anguish over family happenings that are out of his control. The narrative starts out with feelings from a child's view of family events and moves through the life cycle while describing feelings about family happenings that become momentous because of their influence on his development as he forges a personal identity around his struggles. The descriptive anguished feelings expressed are not clinical but rather they are real, raw, genuine, authentic words that David crafts as an emotional catharsis to relieve his intense repression that unconsciously held down these deep feelings from overwhelming him over and again. Towards the end of the book, David embraces his struggles for making him strong over his traumatic past and wrought the freedom that he has sought for his whole life. His experiences of overcoming exemplifies Spurgeon's quote "Many men owe the grandeur of their lives to their tremendous difficulties."

Only a small number of people have put into a narrative account their personal feelings about family, fathers, death and life as real and intensely as David has accomplished; and then beyond exposing deep felt responses from his soul, he bravely takes a springing jump to publish that valuable work in the hopes that it will help others. Along with a clinical Abnormal Psychology text, I Walked the Darkest Valleys to Freedom may be used as an auxiliary supplement that colorfully expresses how it feels to be depressed through a personal account of living with depression. Mental health professionals, patients in mental hospitals, families with mental health problems, military personnel, college students, people with suicidal thoughts and anyone needing emotional health and healing would benefit from reading this book.

Not having computer skills or a technologically advanced computer; David wrote his entire book on a thumb drive. This accumulated treasury of expressed painful feelings and memories is where I came in to this literary gold mine six years ago. I offered to help him organize this writing and brought the paper copy of the manuscript to him; leaving some suggestions on what he needed to do if he wanted to publish it. One year later he sent me the manuscript having made the improvements that I suggested. I live in Fridley MN and David lives in Harlan Iowa and for 6 years we have communicated back and forth by email and thumb drive to put this book into print.

Along with his emotional suffering, and also contributing to his overwhelming feelings, David earned a Master's degree in Audiology, became an Audiology Fellow, developed an audiology program in a school district that did not have one, managed audiology services in 50 schools in AEA13 in Iowa, served on various boards in his community, transformed an inhabitable house into a habitable home, nurtured his marriage to his very dear wife of 54 years; raised a loving family with 3 children subsequently with grandchildren and great grandchildren, worked 1-2 jobs during his teen years to provide for his mother and sister; struggled with depression over his 78 years, had 3 near death experiences, 3 psych ward hospitalizations, a Medtronic Pain Control Stimulator surgery as a result of near death accident, learned how to forgive others and accept forgiveness, developed the spiritual growth plan of daily reading the Bible and spending time in prayer, all the while trying to keep angry and suicidal feelings under control which he succeeded in doing.

I am David's first cousin; our fathers were brothers. My career has been as a college professor at various private colleges and community colleges teaching Educational Psychology, Child Development, Early Childhood Methods, Human Relations, Marriage and Family, Death and Dying, Faith Development, Supervising Student Teachers, and Parenting. I worked with

David by editing his writing, and it was motivating to me because I saw a book coming out of this effort. I endorse this valuable book with joy.
Elaine Pedersen Gunderson EdD


David's Degrees
**BS,MS,CCC-A.A.A.**
**BS and MS Bachelor's and Master's of** Science
C.C.C. Certificate of Clinical Competency Audiology
A.A.A. American Academy of Audiology Fellow

# INTRODUCTION

I must state at the outset that I am neither a physician, psychiatrist, psychologist, nor a counselor or therapist. What I am is one who has been somewhat of a "prodigal son" with painful memories of a troubled past. What I am attempting to convey in this endeavor is a snapshot of my journey through valleys and insurmountable canyons of utter despair to a sense of healing and relief from the accompanying pain on a long and arduous journey. My journey at times has been difficult, painful, and circuitous, and yet also pleasant and peaceful.

I would be remiss if I did not mention the importance of a multi-level intervention approach to healing. I strongly believe that such an intervention program for those suffering with depression, like myself, must include three areas. One essential area should be appropriate psychopharmacological treatment when professionally indicated. Another should be psychiatry and counseling. The third and most essential area is spiritual life, a person's relationship to God; a faith that provides the adhesive to cement everything together. "Grace that does not change my life will not save my soul" (Charles Spurgeon). I discovered that without a Christian persuasion based on God's Holy Word I found myself in a situation similar to treading water where I was temporarily not drowning; but I was not getting anywhere. Regarding faith, Ray Van Der Lan proclaimed that, "Part of the problem in our western culture is that it has not been shaped and controlled by those who hold the same value system we Christians do. As long as that happens we may win some individual skirmishes here and there; but humanly speaking we cannot have" the spiritual vitality in our faith that we need to have to overcome painful memories. The only lasting foundation on which to build a life everlasting is faith in Jesus Christ.

This book project is really the product of one of my therapy sessions. My therapist at the time suggested that it might be beneficial and therapeutic if I would write down or journal concerning my feelings, emotions, actions, behaviors, and thoughts for the day. She was correct in thinking such an endeavor would be therapeutic. Then she indicated that my own journaling notes might make for a good book that could comfort and encourage others. She attributed her support of my writing to my authenticity in sharing my depressed feelings and faith to overcome them. It then occurred to me that a written product such as this might also be beneficial to others experiencing a similar journey. Therefore the motivating force influencing my effort to write this book is my hope that the finished product will indeed fulfill a need that my therapist so prophetically had suggested.

The chapter titles are carefully thought through to capture my feelings that correspond to the events that were happening in my life. The story of my life is a whole, but can be read by picking out individual chapters that may have more meaning to the reader at a particular time.

I would really enjoy hearing from someone who has found some degree of comfort or healing after reading my life story.

I can be reached at jdpedersen@harlannet.com or
David Pedersen,
1219 Baldwin,
Harlan, Iowa 51537

# ACKNOWLEDGEMENTS

Without the editing, encouragement, keeping me on task, and Christian influence by my cousin Elaine, this book would have never come to fruition. Thank you Elaine for all your help in completing this project. Thank you to her daughter who introduced me to the Medtronic Pain Stimulator and helped with the formatting of my book.

My family played a tremendous role in my journey. Without my family's love, devotion, compassion, continued support and patience from my loving wife Judy, our two daughters, Angela and Sheila, and our son Joshua, my journey may very well have taken a very different route. I don't just love you all. I love you more!

With great appreciation and humility, I acknowledge the superb professional quality of services the doctors, nurses, counselors, and therapists have provided to me. It has been a life saver and the rudder keeping my ship on course during my journey to freedom. I acknowledge from my heart with profound gratitude that I sensed your personal caring beyond expectations which was applied to my needs. I highly value your efforts to be the lifeline I needed. Thank you so much!

Thank you Lorna for reading and giving helpful comments on the book. Our new photographer in Harlan, Iowa, Mike Wohlhutter, added the image of Christ to the front cover photograph of David and Josh. Thank you Mike.

# TABLE OF CONTENTS

# Chapter 1
## Valleys of Despair Created By The Hammer of Emotional Pain and the Chisel Of Trauma

Following my mother's suicide, over the next subsequent years, I began to plan my own. Some years later when the traumas of my past were unbearable, I became suicidal and my family had to admit me to the nearest emergency psych ward. After 60 plus years of unresolved loss, grief, anger and despair I found myself in a psych ward no longer able to cope with the pains of losses, rejection and other related issues in my life. One would think with multiple college degrees and successful work experience I would be able to figure some of these things out on my own! For me that was not the case.

For my own protection I was placed at Mercy Hospital once in Council Bluffs, Iowa, and on two other occasions admitted to Heritage House in Omaha, Nebraska; a separate area of Immanuel Hospital for individuals in need of psychiatric care. The doctors and staff determined that I had been over medicated and needed to be detoxified because I had become addicted to some of the narcotic pain medication from a near fatal injury; and secondly I should have been seen quite some time ago for psychiatric care and therapy because of my troubled and painful past. They took away all my medications cold turkey that first night and I thought I would have to get better to die.

How did I get to this point? For my own healing I wrote this book. Hopefully the reader will find my answers to this significant question, and maybe some of their own in the following pages. I offer a child's eye view of family traumas and how I learned the ways that adults handle them. The unfolding of my depression and suicidal thoughts is re-created in the following pages as I tell my life story. For me, that first hammer was early in my development while being separated from my father because of World War II.

# Chapter 2
# WWII Valley of Separation from My Father and Hammer of my Mother's Grief at an Early Age Causes Enduring Feelings of Insecurity and Anxiety

I can remember as a child my mommy saying, "Daddy has to go away for a while." As she spoke those words the expression on her face was that of someone who had just entered that unwanted painfully dark area we know as very deep sadness and grief. The tears that had long been welling up in her eyes were now cascading down her cheeks and slowly dripping on my innocent face. I had seen mommy sad before and even crying. But somehow this situation seemed different. There seemed to be deep down inside her soul a type of sadness causing much tearful trembling and anguish. The Native American expression "Yah Ta Hey" applied to the occasion of my daddy's deployment explains an emotional good-bye to someone very dear who is going away; and at the same time realizing all the feelings of loss, great sadness, grief and anguish, should the person never return. All the emotions and feelings that one would experience in such a situation were present and so intense and so overwhelming that they produced an outpouring of unexpected actions and emotions. That was the atmosphere the day Daddy left. "There is a war and Daddy is needed" mommy said. "Since we do not know how long Daddy will be gone we must pray that God will guide and protect Daddy and return him safely back to us." Mommy's favorite words of comfort were Psalms. "I lift my eyes unto the hills—where does my help come from? It comes from the Lord" (Psalm 121:1-2)( RSV

Bible, 1952). "But make everyone rejoice who puts his trust in you, O God. Keep them shouting for joy because you are defending them. Fill all who love you with your happiness. For you bless the godly man, O Lord; you protect him with your shield of love" (Psalm 5).

The hammer of insecurity and separation from my father caused emotional feelings, fears, and thoughts that created a painful wound. This was truly one of those "Yah-Ta-Hey" moments. This was but one painful hammer of many more to come as part of a long, circuitous, and arduous journey that took me to unwanted, undeserved, desperate, lonely places, situations, events, and experiences in my development that later I desperately tried to escape. Sometimes I was taken to places where I did not want to go; did things I did not want to do, and was kept longer than I wanted to stay. The results of which will forever have an impact on me, my life, my family, and anyone with whom I have associated, and will associate socially and professionally. Some of the valleys were deep and long; some were shallow, steep, and short but all seemingly impossible from which to escape. Regardless of the size or severity of the valley, it is Hope that we have to hold on to. This valley was one of deep sadness with countless episodes of concern, worry, anxiety, fear and questions with answers to be revealed and circumstances yet to be explained.

Daddy left, and to me it seemed as though he would never come home again. I think Mommy felt the same. Mommy received letters from Daddy and read each and every one to me. She kept all of them wrapped with a ribbon and put them in a special place. Then one day she received a special message from Daddy called a "telegram." It said he was being transferred from a place called Fort Carson, Colorado to some place in Tennessee.

Even as a child, I could sense things were not going well. Mommy spent much time listening to the news on the radio. We started having difficulty purchasing things because we were required to have something called "Rationing Stamps and Meat Tokens." When Mommy would meet with other ladies they would talk about the war and their husbands, sons, dads, other relatives and friends. Sometimes some of them would be crying;

4

Mommy and the other ladies would pray, and try to comfort them, and help them not to be so sad. All the ladies would have their little books with the "Rationing Stamps" in them and they would trade with each other so they would have the correct stamps for what they needed to purchase. We even had to have stamps for the gas station to get gas for our car.

Other kids would also be there and we would play while the ladies were busy with their books. Sometimes Mommy and the other ladies would have us kids help them sort certain items that needed to be saved for the war effort. We would put things in piles and boxes. There were stacks of newspapers, boxes of tin cans and glass bottles; and we even had to save orange peels which were somehow used to make explosives.

One other boy, Inky and I became good friends. We played a lot together. I don't recall his real name. Everyone just called him Inky. One day while Inky and I were playing outside, even though I was too young to understand it at the time, I would be the recipient of what I would call a "divine intervention." Somehow Inky and I had wandered near the railroad tracks. Just as I was about to step onto the track to cross to the other side into the path of an oncoming train the station manager from the train depot reached out with his big hands, seemingly from out of nowhere, and grabbed me and pulled me to safety. Words of gratitude from my mother to the depot agent that day could not be adequately expressed and I received my just reward!

One day Mommy got another special letter from Daddy. As she read it I could tell it was important. The sad look on her face began to appear again; but was soon replaced with a big smile. It was another "Yah Ta Hey" moment! There were also tears again, but not like last time. She said, "We're going to see Daddy." The message read: COME IF YOU CAN - MAY SHIP OUT SOON. Immediately she began to pack things in boxes and suitcases. She called some of her lady friends to see if she could trade some of her rationing stamps for gas stamps. Because it was going to be a long trip from Minnesota to Tennessee we would need enough stamps for gas to make the trip. In a couple days Mommy had our stuff packed, loaded in the car, and was able to trade enough rationing stamps to get the amount of gas she thought we would need.

Mommy drove for a very long time. Since Mommy had packed some food in a box we only stopped for gas and potty breaks. Mommy would say in her usual calm voice, "just relax, play with your toys, or sing Mommy a song." She loved to sing and had a very good singing voice. She would say, "I'll get us there as soon as I can." After what seemed an eternity, we finally arrived in Halls Tennessee, but only for a short time; then on to Dyersberg, Tennessee. Mommy and Daddy were very glad to see each other. I didn't think they would ever stop kissing and hugging one another, truly a "Yah Ta Hey" moment. Daddy picked me up and hugged me too. He hugged me so tight I thought I was going to poop or pee in my new underwear!

Winter and the Christmas Season came while we were there. One evening there was just a light skiff of snow that covered the ground. The snowflakes with the light of a full moon reflecting its light seemed to take on the sparkling beauty and brilliance of millions and millions of small ever glowing diamonds. Daddy said, "Let's go get a Christmas tree." Daddy drove us out into the country where there was a good stand of pine trees not far from the road. We walked through the snow from the day before. As we walked through the snow toward the pine trees the little brightly shining diamond-like snowflakes were so brilliant they appeared to automatically brighten as we walked, and in doing so seemed to light a path to one small tree among the large stand of other larger pine trees. Daddy said, "This looks like a good one, what do you think, should we take this one?" We all agreed and Daddy proceeded to chop it down. We took it home and decorated it with things we made. Mommy popped popcorn that we put on string and wrapped around the tree. Decorations cut from paper and other materials were also hung on the tree. The tree had no Christmas tree lights because we couldn't afford them; and even if we would have been able to purchase them I don't think they were available because of the war. But the little tree was beautifully adorned anyway. The Spirit of Christ and the Season of Christmas was in the air regardless of the times.

Daddy was eventually transferred to Dover Airbase in Dover, Delaware. We lived nearby in Willmington, Delaware. There were mixed emotions about Dad being transferred to Dover Airbase because of a general understanding that if you were transferred to Dover airbase, for most, it would be the end of the line. Every day men would stand in line waiting their turn to read lists of names to see if their name was listed. The list was called "Overseas Shipping Duty Roster." If their name was on the list it meant they would be given orders to be shipped overseas to fight in the war.

One day Daddy got permission to take us on base and show us around. Boy, that was a big place and there were people running around everywhere. There were funny looking little cars that Daddy called Jeeps, there were cars, trucks big and small, and airplanes. I had never seen anything as big as those airplanes. Daddy took us to a huge building that looked like a giant garage. Daddy said it was called a hangar and that is where they would put the airplane so they could work on it. There was one of those great big giant airplanes next to that big garage. Daddy called it a B-17 and said "Come on, I'll show you the inside." The door was not very big and it was kind of funny watching Mommy try to get in. She was wearing a dress and almost showed her underwear. One of Daddy's friends lifted me up through the little doorway to get in. Inside all I could see were pipes, tubes, wires and guns— big guns. There wasn't a real floor to walk on. To get to the front or back you had to walk on big pipes. I had trouble walking on them because my feet kept slipping off the pipes and I almost fell down. The front looked like the dash of our 1937 Ford except it was a whole lot bigger with a lot more dials and gauges and stuff. When we got to the little door to get out, Daddy's friend again lifted me down and put me back on the ground. Then he said, "Hey Pete, this thing needs to be checked out; will you do that?" Daddy said, "sure" and turning toward mommy said "Hey honey, do you want to go along?" Mommy agreed and with me standing by on the runway, Daddy's friend shut the little door. When Daddy started those big motors on that big plane they made such a big terrible roar I got scared. I think the ground even started to shake. Then when they got even louder the plane started to move and pretty soon it was going faster and faster down that great big driveway. As I stood there watching that great big airplane with my Mommy and Daddy taking off I thought they were gone forever, and I will never see them again; I began to cry. I wanted them back! Daddy's friend picked me up, held me tight, and told me everything will be fine; they will be back in just a few minutes. Sure enough, pretty soon that big plane circled around and landed. Boy, was I ever glad to see them again.

One day Daddy took us for a ride in the car. He drove us to a huge boat as big as a house that was called a ferry. It was mostly flat and cars were on it, and Daddy like the others drove right up on it and parked the car. People used it to cross Chesapeake Bay to the other side and back again. During our ride across the water Daddy took us to an area of the big boat called a Concession Stand and bought me some licorice and coffee for Mommy and himself. On another day we walked along a beach. We found some really unusual seashells that we kept for souvenirs. We also found what once was a live lobster. It scared me so much that I would not go near it or even touch it.

Eventually the inevitable day came. When it was Daddy's turn in line to check the "Overseas Shipping List" there it was, Harold Pedersen. The next few days were filled again with that deep sadness, tears, anxiety, the awful fear of the unknown, and preparations were made to return home to Minnesota. For Mommy and me the painful, emotional, tear-filled, "Yah Ta Hey" moment of saying goodbye had come once again. After the painful emotional goodbyes we started the long trek back to Minnesota.

After finally arriving home in Minnesota we stayed in Fairmont with Grandpa and Grandma Pedersen temporarily until we could find a house. We finally ended up on North Main Street. There was a huge yard in which to play, and of course Mommy always had a big garden. As the man of the house, so to speak, part of my responsibility was to help with the garden. That was a task I would later learn to dislike a great deal. I would rather be playing or fishing, and when older hunting, trapping, and working on cars. I also liked to go down the street to the house on the corner. Some boys had pet rabbits and I was fascinated by them and loved to watch and hold them.

Why do I mention such an early part of my childhood? The reason I am being autobiographical and chronological is because emotions and feelings caused by adverse situations can become part of one's personality and responses presently and later in life. For some individuals they can pile up adding one onto another like an interest bearing bank account except that the results are not always beneficial. This accumulation of emotions and feelings will become more clear throughout this book. The fallout of the hammering emotions can produce fertile soil and psychological wounds that have far reaching deep seated roots. These roots can sprout and take hold very early in life. Roots, developed at a young age, may not immediately reveal any visible evidence of injury to the feelings, but later they may become deep emotional wounds that affect one's well-being. These unhealed wounds can eventually lead to emotional misery, serious consequences, painful relationships, and even thoughts of suicide. They may not even reveal their presence until much later after they have become twisted beyond recognition. In my case it was severe clinical depression that after many years would eventually rear its ugly head.

What do I mean by emotional pain? Wounds? It is easy to understand physical pain like "hurting" in contrast to emotional pain. Using the hammer analogy, we can see the swelling, bruising, bleeding, or some physical evidence of a wound from the hammer. We can experience emotional, mental, psychological discomfort, hurt or pain as well as the physical form. Emotional pain is anxiety, mental distress, uneasiness about future uncertainties, fear lacking a specific cause, agonizing anguish, emotional wounds or suffering as a result of emotional trauma or unresolved grief, all of which may be more painful than physical pain. The visible evidence of emotional trauma and a long walk through the darkest valley of emotional wounds from a psychological hammer may not be immediately present. Whether feelings or emotions seem positive or negative, good or bad, they can wound like hammers even though they may be invisible. These diseased feelings may appear later and cause an array of life altering behaviors and actions.

# Chapter 3
## Starting a New Life after WWII Looks Good

Erma, one of my mother's younger sisters, and her son Billy Lee would visit quite often. Her husband Bill was also away because of the war. Billy Lee and I played together almost constantly when they came to visit. We were only a couple months apart in age and almost inseparable. We were more like brothers than we were cousins. The bonding that took place between us would continue even as we got older, and would one day become a welcome and needed oasis in the desert location of one of my many painful valleys. I cherish that bonding even to this day even though Billy Lee has since passed away. Grieving his loss is still a painful emotional valley.

It was 1945, the war was finally over and Daddy was home in Fairmont, MN. He got a job as an auto mechanic at Colvins Pontiac dealership and later at Park Motors, the Ford dealership in town. Things were going quite well. We moved from the house on North Main Street to a little house on Hall Lake. Now we had an easy access to enjoy our fishing. It was more like a little cottage than a house, but it was perfect for us. It even had a real fireplace. You could walk out the back door and down a slight hill and you were at our boat dock. Next to the dock was a boathouse except we didn't have a boat, at least not yet. As for modern conveniences we only had electricity and running water. We didn't mind making the trek to the little shack out back, we were used to that. Later when we got an indoor chemical toilet we thought that was real special. Now we didn't have to make any more trips outside to the little shack out back even in the dead of winter. That was especially nice during the cold Minnesota winters. The only problem was where the chemical toilet had to be located. The only space available was on the porch. Needless to say timing was critical!

# Chapter 4
## Trauma of Christmas Eve 1945 Fire Memory, and the Frustrating Toy Caterpillar with an Unwanted Twist

Christmas Eve that December of 1945, Mom and I, Erma and Billy Lee went to see Ardis, another younger sister, and her husband Arva to deliver Christmas gifts. Like Dad, Arva was now home from the war awaiting his separation papers. It was cold and had snowed so we had to walk through snow to get to the house. Arva had not yet had time to shovel the snow because he had been busy trying to light the oven on their gas stove. With the next day being Christmas Day they had planned to have roast turkey for dinner. Meanwhile Billy Lee and I were fascinated with Uncle Arva and the oven lighting ordeal; while Mom, Erma, and Ardis were busy with gift wrapping and Christmas decorations. The oven just would not light. It was getting to be quite a procedure. Turn on the gas, set the dial, light a match and place it where it was to light the oven. The match would go out, turn off the gas, get another match ready, turn on the gas, reset the dial, light the match, place it where it was to light the oven, and out goes the match. I don't know how many times he tried or how many matches he went through; but by now Billy Lee and I were right down there in the action watching and waiting with hopeful anticipation for that magic moment when the magic match would finally get the oven to light. All of a sudden there was a tremendous blast, the oven door blew open, and I think it was even blown off its hinges. Out rushed hot air, fire, and smoke with such force, Billy Lee and I ended up across the kitchen seated on the floor against the opposite wall. Apparently enough gas had accumulated during the lengthy lighting procedure to cause the explosion. Probably in a state of shock we didn't even realize that we had been injured from the exploding oven. While fire was now spreading rapidly with reckless abandon to the rest of the house; Mom and Erma instinctively grabbed us and practically threw us outside into a snow bank with only the smelly somewhat charred clothes we were wearing. Then they frantically rushed back into the house, called the fire department, and the four of them began the losing battle of trying to extinguish what became a blazing inferno. The four luckily escaped with the clothes they were wearing, singed hair and only minor burn injuries when the firemen arrived. The firemen frantically tried to stop the blazing inferno but to no avail. The home was a total loss. The next thing I remember is terrible excruciating pain with the doctor removing burned skin from my face and right hand and arm with forceps while Mom was trying her best to calm and comfort a screaming child out of control. When the doctor was finally finished, my face and right hand and arm were all wrapped in white gauze and bandages. I looked like a one handed mummy!

For Christmas the next day, one of the gifts I received was a little metal wind-up toy caterpillar. When I wound it up and moved a little lever the caterpillar would creep along the floor. It even had a blade in the front that could be moved up and down. I tried to wind it up to make it go; but being right handed, and because of my hand being wrapped, and the pain of trying to do so; I was unable to wind it up. Out of frustration and some resulting pain and anger, I threw it across the room. Like me, it too was now slightly damaged. Some of the metal was bent and the blade on the front was a little askew; but when Mom or Dad wound it up, it still worked. I played with that toy caterpillar for many years until it finally went to the great toy box in the sky!

That is what I remember of that Christmas Eve of 1945 in our little cottage on Hall Lake on Albion Avenue. The burns heal and life goes on. I still have some remaining physical evidence in the form of scars on my right hand and arm, and if I don't shave for two or more days it's obvious I have less to shave on the right side of my face than I do on the left. We were so fortunate we were not more seriously injured. Also, with how rapidly the fire spread, it is miraculous no lives were lost. The emotional and psychological wounds of that fateful night were added to the separation scars and memories from WWII that still linger as though it was still Christmas Eve 1945 so many years ago.

That event created somewhat of an interesting twist many years later. The pastor and his wife of the church we were attending at that time invited my wife and I and a few other church members to a Christmas coffee at their home. During the visiting, the pastor asked each of us what first comes to mind when we hear the word Christmas. Obviously there were the usual responses of the virgin Mary, birth, birth of Christ, birth of Jesus, being born in a stable; the wisemen, shepherds, and angels. But when it came my turn I responded with "caterpillar!" Everyone including the pastor was, needless to say, somewhat shocked. I too had the same thoughts as everyone else; but since the pastor had specifically asked for the first thing that came to mind when they heard the word Christmas, I felt obligated to be honest and truthful so I had to say "caterpillar." I then had to explain why; and told them about the event that occurred in 1945 on that fateful Christmas Eve so many years ago. The pastor indicated how he thought it interesting that earlier events can shape and have an effect on a person's emotions, feelings, and thoughts later in life. My personal unspoken response was that it was just one more evidence of unwanted, out of my control, memorable experiences traveling with me through life.

# Chapter 5
## Lies and the Stolen Cap Gun Leave Uneasy feelings

Now that the war had been over for a few years, and seemingly having
rather nomadic tendencies, we made a couple more moves from Minnesota.
The first was to West Des Moines, Iowa, which as I recall, was rather short
lived. I don't know the details but I think it was a situation where an idea
was hatched among Dad and his war buddies whereby they would go into
partnership repairing cars and trucks. Knowing my Dad was an excellent
mechanic and body and fender repairman, and a good businessman; I think
the other guys probably thought of it as a way to continue their camaraderie
and earn an income at the same time. Unfortunately, I think it turned out to
be a case where Dad did all or most of the work, while the others still
expected their share of the profits, which would eventually add a feeling of
vulnerability to my wounds. At such an early age I was feeling my dad's
uneasiness, the injustice of it, and trying to understand the situation.

Even though still a child I had a rather unfortunate experience with the
local law enforcement there in West Des Moines. I was playing cowboys
and Indians by myself in front of Dad's shop. It was a hot summer day and
because of the furious battle going on, I and those under my command
were soaking wet with perspiration! Being totally involved in my own self-
proclaimed Cowboy and Indian war, and boldly defending the
make-believe fort with my one trusty six-shooter cap gun, I was unaware of
the lone stranger approaching from the south. As the lone hombre got
closer, I happened to notice he was about my age and about my size, maybe

a little heavier. He said, "Hi! Can I see your cap gun?" Since it was time to reload anyway; I agreed knowing full well this would provide my attacking enemy ample time to intensify his attack by placing my imaginary fort at risk of being totally overtaken. As a result, there would probably be no survivors. After handing him my six shooter he immediately turned and began running south from whence he came. I instantly declared a truce since I no longer had a weapon with which to fight and began chasing the little thief who just stole my cap gun! As I chased him down the street he began screaming bloody murder as though some blood thirsty bounty hunter was hot on his trail. Earlier I had seen a policeman walking north on the other side of the street and didn't think he would be of much use at this point. I was closing in on that hombre of a thief and had already forgotten about the policeman. Suddenly, seemingly out of nowhere, there was that policeman standing between me and the escaping thief causing me to immediately stop in my tracks. Looking down at me with his hands on his hips, and giving me a stern look he said "Why are you chasing my son?" With a lump in my throat as big as a basketball I tried to respond but nothing would come out. At that point I'm the one screaming bloody murder running back to Dad's shop totally petrified, and hoping I can quickly find him to save me from prosecution and certain incarceration. Hearing me cry, and thinking something very serious had happened, Dad and I practically collided as I entered the shop trembling from fear and out of breath with sweat running down my face from my speedy retreat. Dad asked me what had happened and why I was crying. Between sobs and gasps for breath I said "He, he, he, stole my cap gun!" "Well," he said, "we better go have a chat with your young friend." With Dad's tall lanky frame over six feet tall, long strides, and me trying my best to keep up and as close as possible, we proceeded south for the showdown as though it was high noon on some old western street. The police officer and his family lived in the apartment above a corner grocery store. Dad and the officer exchanged pleasantries and general conversation and he finally said to the officer, "It seems your son and my son have something to settle" as though the young thief and I were waiting to see who was going to draw his six-shooter cap gun first. The only problem is that I was now totally unarmed because he still had my one and only trusty cap gun! The officer turned to me and said with his deep booming voice "What's the problem son?" With a lump in my throat again I finally said, "Uh, he, he, took my cap gun!" "ADAM," he said in a gruff and loud booming voice that could probably be heard in the next zip code "COME HERE!" Adam slowly appeared, head downcast, hands clasped behind his back while trying to hide something. Adam's father asked him in his stern police officer voice, "Did you take David's cap gun?" After a brief pause Adam slowly replied "Yes sir, I did!" "Then give it back," his father said loudly. Adam slowly handed me my six shooter cap gun and quietly said, "Here. I'm sorry I took your cap gun." Dad and the officer shook hands and as we turned to leave the officer said to me, "I'm sorry if I frightened you son!" I placed my cap gun back into my holster and Dad and I returned to the shop and the car he was working on. I returned to my imaginary fort to see if the truce declared earlier had held, or if the fort had been overtaken leaving few if any survivors!

Adam and I played together a couple times after the cap gun incident; but never really became close friends. I played more often with a young black boy named Sammy who lived behind us across the alley near the "goat lady's" house. I never knew his last name or where he lived. He would crawl through a hole in a wooden fence past the alley to come over to play. He was rather quiet and he never stayed very long. It was as if he was either afraid of being there or afraid of being punished for being away from home.

# Chapter 6
## Fire and the Goat Lady Mystery

The "Goat Lady's" house was the talk of the neighborhood. Her house was a large imposing two story frame house with a full sized attic. The house was across the alley to the west and a block or two south. It was said she had goats and other animals living with her in the house. None of the animals were ever seen but people were convinced they were there. About the only time she was ever seen in public was when she would get groceries from Spencer's Grocery store. One day tragedy struck. The Goat Lady's house caught fire. The fire department was called and there was a frantic attempt to save her and her animals, and to extinguish the blazing inferno. Tragically she died in the fire. My Dad was the one who tried to help extinguish the inferno, and examined the charred aftermath. There were no goats or animals. One thing obviously evident was a huge pile of charred and semi-charred books. The elderly lady who was being wrongly accused of being the "Goat Lady" was a lonely, eccentric, very well educated person dying a tragic death from a fire in her own home like an unknown soldier; sadly and tragically killed in action!

## Chapter 7
## Dad the Mechanic's Mechanic was Dogged by Inadequate Finances, Dad Gave Me the Love of Working with him in his Shop

We made move number eight to a small town in northern Iowa, called Armstrong, only 20 miles south of my hometown of Fairmont, Minnesota. This would be the last move we would make as a family. Dad opened a shop in an old gas station on the edge of town. It wasn't much but it would do. The garage part was just big enough for two cars if you were careful. There was a small office adjacent to the garage and gas pumps out front. He sold Mobil gas, repaired anything with an engine, and did body and fender repair as well as painting. Above the shop, we lived in a large one room apartment. As for modern conveniences we were back to only electricity and running water. Heat in the winter came through an opening in the floor from the shop below. Dad worked long and hard in his shop struggling to make ends meet. It was not uncommon to find him still working late into the night to finish the jobs he was working on. He was also gone on many weekends either on a tow-truck service call or looking at wrecked cars to rebuild.

He was extremely good at what he did. He had excellent problem solving skills. He had a special gift at being able to figure out what was wrong with a car and was able to make the necessary repair. He was a mechanic's mechanic and a body and fender repairman's repairman. He had an uncanny ability that many yearn, work, and strive for but few ever achieve. During my lifetime I know of only three with such a mechanical gift, or ability. My father was the first. My late nephew Matt was the second; and the third is a man in the town in which we currently live. It was amazing to watch my Dad work with his ever persistent surgeon-like precision. If he could not fix it, it could not be fixed. I recall one particular night when Dad worked late, because this was different from many others. He had been working on a car for days that had a problem which seemed impossible to fix. The owner had brought his car to Dad in desperation because he had taken it to numerous garages with nothing to show for it, but bills for labor and no results. The owner said, "the darn thing just won't accelerate. It goes so slow I can count fence posts!" Dad had checked all the usual things like electronics, ignition, gas, fuel pump, fuel lines, carburetor and everything proved to be in good working order. He was really bewildered. He stood there for the longest time looking really perplexed, and was wondering if he might yet be another of the past failures. But being the perceptive and persistent person he was he pressed on. He checked and rechecked everything he had previously checked to make sure he had not missed something when suddenly he had that "Aha-moment" look on his face. He quickly reached for some wrenches and proceeded to remove one of the exhaust manifolds from the engine. After removing the exhaust manifold he took a piece of welding rod, and after fashioning a hook on the end he began to probe the exhaust ports. Finally, after searching three of the four exhaust ports on one side, with a little difficulty from the fourth, out came the "butterfly" from the heat-riser valve. The heat-riser valve is a spring loaded mechanism bolted between the exhaust manifold and the exhaust pipe. Its function when closed was to temporarily trap the initial heat from the exhaust of the engine to help the engine warm more quickly to its normal operating temperature. The spring on the heat-riser valve was weighted. As the heat from the exhaust warmed the spring it would weaken and the weight would cause the valve, or "butterfly," to open and keep it open while the engine continued to run and in doing so allows the exhaust to pass through the exhaust system and out the tail pipe.

Apparently at some time the engine had backfired with so much force that the "butterfly" broke free and was sucked into one of the exhaust ports of the engine. As a result, the engine was unable to expel all of the burned and unburned gasses causing loss of power and therefore was unable to accelerate. Dad quickly reassembled what he had removed and took the car for a test drive. It was a complete success. The car performed perfectly and had speed to spare. I don't know for sure, but I suspect before turning the car over to its owner he performed a little magic of his own, which he always did to every car that came into the shop. I do not know what exactly he did whether it was electrical, ignition, timing, carburetion or a combination thereof, but the end result was always an improvement in performance. The customer would always come back and say, "Pete, I don't know what you did but my car has more zip than it ever had." This was my Daddy! He could fix anything!

When bored, I would often wander into the shop looking for something to do; or get into something that I shouldn't be getting into. Dad would never get angry with me for being in his way or being a general pest. Instead, he would redirect me to a task of some kind he knew would keep me occupied. He kept a large box on a shelf under his workbench that was full of carburetors and fuel pumps removed from vehicles he had worked on. He would say, "grab one of those fuel pumps or carburetors out of that box under the bench, take it apart and put it back together for me." That proved to be one of his most used diversions and most enjoyable for me. It was probably the beginning of a love affair for working not only on cars, but anything mechanical which I still enjoy to this day many years later. That seemingly simple act of diversion turned out to be a very intuitive lesson for me as I got older. It taught me to be attentive to detail, the importance of sequence, creativity, persistence, patience, and the ability to develop good problem solving skills. The Apostle Paul wrote that we each have our own special gift from God of one kind or another. Dad certainly had a gift. For a man who never graduated from high school he certainly was a remarkable man and would have been remarkable even if he did graduate!

I also remember when he devised a way for Grandpa Cassem to operate the dimmer switch on his car by hand. Grandpa's car was a 1938 Ford with the dimmer switch on the floor. Grandpa had lost a leg in a farming accident years ago so he was unable to operate the floor mounted dimmer switch. Dad also converted the manual brakes to hydraulic brakes on Grandpa's car.

My Dad was also a compassionate man. After the war, he sponsored a family that had become refugees as a result of the war. He gave the man a job and helped him to find a place for his family to live until they could be on their own. I also remember on two occasions he took in families for shelter after being stranded by a winter blizzard.

I remember dad with so much affection and admiration. He was my hero, and as I grew older I tried to emulate him in many ways. I never will be over six feet tall and have big feet like he did, but I tried to fill bigger shoes the way he did.

Of the many cars he repaired I remember one in particular. It was a dark green 1949 Buick Roadmaster. It had been hit by a train broadside while crossing a railroad track. The whole passenger side was caved in and the car really looked destined for the junk yard. The car was at our place because Dad also had a tow-truck service and he had towed the car from the accident scene. I guess he thought if he could buy it at the right price, knowing what it would cost to repair it, he would either repair it and resell it, or maybe keep it as a family car. It was a Buick Roadmaster four door sedan, and other than the damage, it was the fanciest car I had ever seen. A car like that was more suited for somebody rich like a banker, lawyer, or doctor. He was able to buy it cheap enough to warrant fixing it up. Over the next few months he began working on that mangled piece rescued from a junk yard. With surgical precision he began to disassemble it down to its bare bones. Not only were the body and doors badly mangled, but the frame was so badly bent it was beyond being repaired. To Dad that seemed a minor detail. He simply ordered a new frame from General Motors! That meant the old frame had to be completely stripped. The body, engine, transmission, rear differential, springs, steering, wheels, wiring, and anything else attached to the frame; everything right down to the last nut and bolt! Dad had some friends help lift off the body and set it temporarily on steel barrels. The frame and chassis were rolled from under the body and the laborious task of stripping the old frame of all its belongings began. All that remained was a mangled Buick body sitting on steel drums and a pile of automotive parts on the floor of the shop. Then one day a big truck arrived with the brand new frame. After the frame was unloaded and placed in the appropriate place he spray painted it black. When the paint was dry he began the process of replacing everything he had removed from the old frame onto the new frame. Once that was completed the frame and chassis were rolled under the still badly mangled body. The body was then gently lowered onto its new frame and secured in place. Dad then began to work on the body. He would pound here and there, use a hydraulic jack here and there, use a cutting and welding torch here and there, replace some parts, repair other parts, and slowly it began to resemble a car again. Finally the Buick Roadmaster was completely reassembled, completely repaired and ready for a new coat of paint. He repainted it the original dark green with a hint of metallic. It was not only gorgeous but truly the work of a master. He would never say so but I think deep down even he was proud of the work he had done.

I don't know how long we had that fine specimen of an automobile, nor do I remember what happened to it, but I suspect Dad eventually sold it to help make ends meet financially. Dad would do this periodically. He would buy what others considered a pile of junk and turn it into a vehicle looking like it had just rolled off the assembly line. He bought, repaired, and resold numerous vehicles this way. With the exception of the Buick, we never had a car of our own for very long.

Dad was a loving provider and did the best he could with what was available. Mom, like Dad, was also a loving, caring, and a nurturing parent. She sewed most of our clothes, and canned a lot of produce from our huge garden. We only went to town to Snyders' General Store when necessary for things we needed, or couldn't get from our garden. Snyder's General Store was much like one you would see in episodes of "Little House On The Prairie" or a western such as "Gunsmoke." As soon as you enter there was a long isle down the center. Partway down the center were bins of cookies, crackers, sugar, flour, and pickles. The floor was of oiled wood boards. On the right side were all the grocery items. On the left was anything that was non grocery such as hardware, sewing supplies, cloth and notions. At the far end of the store was a potbelly stove, and hanging above on the wall was a shotgun and some traps. In the back room Mr. Snyder had large wooden barrels of vinegar and pickles. To this day I can still smell the oiled wooden floor, and visualize all the items the way they were displayed in the store.

By today's standards I guess one would have to say we were poor but we didn't know it, and even if we did it didn't matter!

# Chapter 8
## Daddy and Mommy Go Hunting and Fishing, We Enjoy Being a Family

Dad was an avid outdoorsman as was my mother. They both enjoyed hunting and fishing. I'm told when they were first married they would go duck hunting together. They could only afford the one used shotgun that Dad had purchased some years prior; only one pair of hip boots, and they had no duck boat. As a result, Dad would carry Mom out to the duck blind. He would then return to the car to get the shotgun and ammunition and wade back to the duck blind and the two of them would share the duck blind as well as the shotgun. When they were finished he would take the shotgun and ducks to the car, and return to the duck blind and again carry Mom back to dry land. I wonder how many couples would do that today? He also enjoyed deer hunting back home in Minnesota. His dream though was to be able to one day go on a hunting trip somewhere to shoot a Moose. But that hunting trip was destined never to happen. Pheasant hunting was usually an annual family affair. We would either be hunting with Dad's brothers and brothers-in-law or with Mom's brothers. My cousins and I would have a great time helping retrieve the birds they shot.

When I was about seven years old Dad surprised me with that old hand-me-down Iver Johnson .410 single shot shotgun. It was not new. In fact it was quite old. It was the infamous hand-me-down family heirloom. My dad's father, my grandfather Andrew, had purchased it many years before. As each of the five Pedersen boys became old enough Grandpa would pass it down for them to hunt and help put food on the table. It ended up in my father's possession and then was given to me. I still have that little .410 and it is still in shootable condition even after nearly 100 years. When I felt our son, Joshua, was old enough I did as my father had done; I passed it on to him to keep it in the family.

When Dad went hunting pheasants he would let me tag along with him while carrying his favorite shotgun, and me carrying my trusty Daisy B-B gun, and later when he thought I was old enough, I would carry the old family hand-me-down .410 single shot shotgun.

I'm told that at about age 14 Dad became such a good shot with that .410 nobody wanted to hunt with him. Men from the cities would come to Grandpa's farm each Fall to hunt pheasants. Word of Dad's shooting ability with that little .410 soon got around and when the men came to hunt they would always ask, "Is Harold going along? We just as soon he not go with us because he gets all the birds!"

# Chapter 9

## At Age Nine I Experienced Anxiety and Uncertainty About the Future as Dad Left for Work in Thule Greenland for Nine Months to Alleviate Our Severe Financial Struggles; Dad Closes his Shop and I Worry; Rosemary is Born

On my eighth birthday our family grew by one. My sister Rosemary was born on my birthday. About a year and a half later my sister Coreen was born. We were now a happy family of five. Financially though things were not all that bright. Sure, Dad was excellent at what he did and was earning an income. With the long hours repairing cars, the wrecker, the occasional rebuilding and resale of wrecked cars; Dad didn't feel he was providing enough for his family. He began thinking of different kinds of work. Since neither Mom nor Dad had graduated from high school, he began taking correspondence courses to further his education. He was realizing that education was becoming increasingly more important. Unfortunately only an occasional correspondence lesson was about all we could afford.

One day a friend of his suggested he look into a government job. An airbase was being built in Thule Greenland. Dad said, "Thule Greenland, where in the world is Thule Greenland?" His friend Cal told him he had already been there twice and was in the process of trying to go back again. Cal went on to explain that the United States had negotiated an agreement with Denmark to build an airbase as part of an early warning defense system. Cal also told him he was pretty sure they could use a good mechanic, and that the pay was really good. He also told Dad that since he was a veteran he didn't think he would have any trouble getting a job there. With Dad still somewhat in a state of shock, I think he said something like, "Yes, but what about my family and my shop?" Cal told him he would be gone for 9 months and then they would send you back home. About closing your shop for nine months; you would make enough so that you would still come out ahead. Well! That was quite a revelation! Dad didn't quite know how to respond. After pondering it awhile, he finally told Mom what Cal had told him. It was a difficult decision for Dad to make I'm sure. He didn't want to leave his family again, but yet he wanted to be able to provide a life for us that would be better than what we were experiencing; even though there were no complaints. I'm sure there were many agonizing evenings of discussion and prayer after we three kids were in bed. I'm also sure that this decision would put the Christian Faith and values of both of them to the ultimate test. For Dad it was a difficult decision to even consider going to Greenland.

It was finally decided he would look into it. Cal helped him get the proper paperwork and the application process began. It wasn't long until a reply was received and his application had been approved. Along with the approval notice was a list of items he would be required to take with him. In addition to the usual personal items was a list of extreme cold weather clothing apparel. One such item was a heavy parka. I think that Mom may have used some money she was saving from the sales of her bumper crop of tomatoes that year to purchase the parka. Anyway all the items were obtained, and now it was a waiting game for the travel orders and tickets to be issued. I would be nine years old later that year. Rosemary and Coreen were too young to understand what was about to take place, but I knew Dad was going to be gone again. I was used to him being gone. But this was a different type of "gone." As Dad's departure for Greenland became more imminent, my fears and anxieties about how I would feel during his absence grew. My memories of the loneliness and insecurity I felt when we were separated during the war came back with unwanted familiarity at my young age.

One issue that caused me considerable anxiety was the thought of Dad closing his shop. What if things didn't turn out as Cal had said? When he returned nine months later would his old faithful customers return or would they take their repair work elsewhere? What if? What if?

The travel orders and tickets finally arrived. All that was left was to say the goodbyes and wait for his departure date. I had no ill feelings about him being gone again. What I was experiencing was the anxiety of him being gone for nine months even though I knew he would be returning. Nine months! For me that was an eternity.

The dread and anxiety at this time, that I wouldn't come to know and wrestle with until many years later as an adult was the beginning of uneasiness, worry, fear and distress about future uncertainties; and the result of no longer experiencing the loving father son bonding in the shop with the fuel pumps and carburetors, walking corn fields for pheasants, playing catch in the back yard, helping me look for good places to set my traps, going fishing, just knowing he was there, and even knowing I would be disciplined when I had done something wrong. It was the beginning of a new reality with which I still struggle to this day some sixty plus years later. Even at this writing it is still such a tender and painful subject adequate words are not available. The native American expression "Yah-Ta-Hey" comes to mind.

# Chapter 10
## Father Absence, Painful Ear Infections, Unfair Teacher, More "Yah Ta Hey" Loneliness

I was also having a problem of my own. I was one of those kids who had to experience and endure chronic ear infections. I would get excruciatingly painful earaches. My eardrums would burst and then my ears would drain. The drainage would cease, my eardrums would heal over and the process would start all over again. Back then there didn't seem to be much that could be done medically so I suffered through it until I was in the fourth grade when the ear trouble seemed to end on its own. Now, as a retired audiologist I fully understand. I have tested and referred for medical treatment hundreds perhaps thousands of children with the same condition. I missed a lot of school during first and second grade, especially first grade. My ear trouble also had an adverse effect on my academic performance which I would later understand as a working professional in the field of hearing health care.

Like many schools back then reading classes were divided into groups. Students were assigned to specific groups based on their reading ability and academic performance. My class had four such reading groups and each group was given a name. I was in the top reading group called the Bluebirds. The bottom group was called the Sparrows.

One of the stories in our reading books which my teacher told us we would actually get to do, was about some students who wanted to do a project of providing food for birds during the Winter. With the town park just across the street from the school it would be easy to take food to the park for the birds. Our class even started to make different things to use for feeding the birds like pinecones with peanut butter rolled in seeds.

Before the Bluebirds got to that story, I began having those severe earaches again. As a result I missed about 2 weeks of school. During that time the Bluebirds got to that story about feeding the birds and the Bluebirds reading group did get to take food for the birds in the park just as the teacher had promised.

When I returned to school I was surprised to learn that the teacher had removed me from the Bluebirds group and placed me in the Sparrows group. I was a little disappointed. But I was looking forward to when the Sparrows group got to the same story where we would be able to go to the park to feed the birds. Much to my astonishment and disappointment, when the Sparrows group did get to the bird feeding story; the teacher announced we would not be going to the park to feed the birds as the others had been able to do. There was no explanation as to why we were not going; it was just that the Sparrows group would not be going. Another wound and valley to add to an already accumulating emotional bank account! The teacher, an authority figure, for unknown reasons changed her mind and did not keep her promise as previously stated. We sparrows were not treated fairly or equally as the other reading groups, an early hammer of damage that seemed unfair!

The evening Dad was to leave for Greenland I was miserable. I had been experiencing another one of those excruciating earaches and draining ears. Mom had me lay on the davenport to see if that would help the pain and possibly I could doze off and take a nap. I did nap for a short time but did awaken from the nagging earaches after awhile. Dad picked me up and sat me on his lap while sitting on one of the dining room chairs, held me tight; and tried to comfort me the best he could. He talked to me about different things trying to divert my thoughts away from thinking about the pain I was experiencing. Little did I know, that evening sitting on his lap would be the last time my father would ever be able to sit with me on his lap and lovingly hold me tight in his arms. This would be the last time I would feel the total security, safety, and strong arms from my dad. I knew I could totally feel like he could take care of anything. He could fix anything. His strong arms could move mountains and protect me at the same time. It was OK to be small, I was safe. Unfortunately things were about to change.

The hour arrived, it was time to leave. We had to travel from Armstrong all the way to the airport in Minneapolis, Minnesota. It was planned that he would fly from Minneapolis to Goose Bay Labrador and from there he would fly to Thule Greenland.

It took hours for us to reach Minneapolis and finally the airport. Then we had to wait while they got the plane ready and all of Dad's stuff loaded along with all the other luggage. Then it was time for another painful "Yah Ta Hey." We said our final goodbyes and Mom, Coreen, Rosemary and I began the long trip back home. I don't know what was going through my mother's mind during that long trip home, but I felt sadly alone and anxious in our new family structure.

Shortly after arriving home we received a telegram from Dad. Apparently his flight out of Minneapolis for some reason was either delayed or cancelled. That meant he would have to wait for the next flight which would be in a couple days. Uncle Bill, Erma's husband offered to drive mom back to Minneapolis so she could see dad one more time before he left for Greenland. Rosemary, Coreen and I stayed with relatives for a couple days while they were gone.

Again Dad was gone and life was certainly different. We missed him terribly. The shop bathroom and our bathroom were one and the same. The shop downstairs was closed and it gave an eerie feeling being down there with it completely void of any cars to be worked on, all of Dad's tools hanging neatly in their places, no whirring thump from a running air compressor; and even the box of fuel pumps and carburetors was neatly tucked away on the shelf under the long workbench. Without Dad it felt cold, empty, lonely, and abandoned. The only sound one could hear was that of an occasional car or truck passing by outside on the highway.

Every week we wrote letters to Dad. Sometimes I would play tricks on him in my letters. One time I wrote the whole letter in a spiral so he would have to keep turning the paper to be able to read the letter. Another time I divided each page into fourths and would mix up the letter by randomly using different fourths as I continued the letter. We would tell him about things going on at home like; so and so's car catching on fire, what Rosemary and Coreen were doing, and me falling out of the top bunk of our bunk bed. I didn't get hurt just shocked by the sudden stop that woke me up. We wrote just about anything we could think of that we thought might be of interest so that he would still feel a part of home even though he was so far away. Of course we always ended each letter telling him how much we loved him, how much we missed him, and to be careful not to get frostbitten from the cold.

Almost every week we would receive a letter from him. He would describe what the place was like. He told us about meeting a couple Eskimos who would occasionally pass through while hunting. He told about two guys he met and how they had become such close friends. One was named Francis S. from Wisconsin, and the other named Eddy E. who was originally from Idaho. He said everyone called Eddy "Shorty," a nickname that fit him perfectly, because he was a real funny character. He even would comment on how fun it was to try to figure out how I had written some of my letters. In one of his letters he wrote about a World War II pilot who had somehow become disoriented, lost, and crashed his plane not too far from the base; but was never found. Sometime after Dad arrived in Greenland the crash site was discovered by Eskimos who were hunting. He said it was like a time capsule frozen in time and a rather eerie sight with the pilot still sitting in the cockpit of the plane as though he was only sleeping. Looking at this in retrospect, I'm sure this sight may have triggered some previous unpleasant WW II memories which he never talked about with anyone not even family.

Since Thule Airbase was a government installation, cameras were not allowed, so at first it took a little imagination to truly grasp what he was writing about. After a couple months, the camera ban was lifted and Dad was then able to send us pictures. He sent pictures of himself with Francis and Shorty and the two Eskimos he met. He also sent pictures of the surrounding landscape showing how barren it looked all covered with ice and snow. It was also very interesting as well as educational to actually be able to see what Greenland really looked like.

After about four months, Dad wrote in one of his letters that he went to see the base doctor because of a swelling in his neck. The doctor said he just had a case of the "Greenland Mumps" and that he would be fine. A couple months later the swelling was still present, and since there had been a change in doctors he decided to see the new doctor for a second opinion. The doctor took one look at Dad and said, "Mister you're going home!" But before being sent home the doctor took a biopsy from the swelling in his neck, and from the lymph gland under Dad's right arm. After arriving home Dad was to see our family doctor.

# Chapter 11

## Father's Traumatic Illness, Unplanned Return From Greenland, Another Separation and Stay with Mom's Relatives Without Explanation, Leaves Unanswered Questions for Me

When we received the message we were, of course, glad that Dad was coming home, but we didn't understand why. He wasn't scheduled to return for another three months. Once he arrived in Minneapolis he surprised us with a telephone call, and said he would take a bus as far as Mankato, and would be at the hotel. Could we please come and get him? Mom and I made the trip to Mankato and located the hotel. The hotel had one of those doors that would open automatically all by itself. I had never seen such a thing. I was really fascinated and wondered how a door could be so smart and open by itself. Every time one approached the doorway and stepped on a certain spot the door would open. I think the man behind the desk was beginning to get irritated with my testing it to see if it worked every time, and indeed it did!

After checking at the main desk and asking for Dad's room number, we proceeded to locate Dad's room. The hotel also had an elevator. Mom pushed a button and soon a door slid open. Inside the elevator was a man sitting on a little stool-like seat. He asked, "What floor please?" and Mom told him which floor. He pushed a couple buttons, pulled a lever, the door slid shut, and we started moving. As we approached the floor of Dad's room the man reached for the lever and began to move it and suddenly, with a slight jerk, we stopped and the door opened. We stepped into the hallway, the door slid shut and the man disappeared. We walked down the hallway to Dad's room and found him resting on the bed. What a joy to once again see Dad. Mom and Dad embraced, kissed, and once again we were together as a family. However, the question still lingered unanswered. Why was he sent home early?

Mom noticed the incision mark from the biopsy on Dad's neck and under his arm. She asked about it and they discussed what the base doctor had told him. Dad was told that our family doctor would take over when he got home.

My family had just suffered and endured another major separation and was adjusting to a new normal while too familiar feelings of fear, loss and anxiety were still fresh in our memories and started to build up again. The direction for our family was out of control with decisions being made without our input. We will later learn that some decisions, in my opinion, seem to have been made without good judgment and lacked understanding of the emotional needs of Rosemary, Coreen and me. This new trauma together with emotions still raw from the last separation caused us to struggle under the hammer again and slip into the dark valley of unanswered questions, anxiety, and fear of what the future holds. This valley had not yet been conquered.

After we arrived home Dad made an appointment to see our family doctor. He checked Dad over very thoroughly, and reviewed the report from the base doctor in Greenland. After a short pause, which was customary for him regardless of who he was seeing, he told Dad he was referring him to the V.A. Hospital in Iowa City, Iowa, and that he would make all the arrangements. Shortly thereafter a letter was received from the V.A. telling Dad the date and time he was to arrive at the hospital, and a reminder to bring his military discharge papers.

At this point, due to circumstances destined to occur, dramatic changes that will affect all of us are beginning to unfold. Because Mom would be accompanying Dad and stay in Iowa City as long as necessary, arrangements were made for my two younger sisters and me to stay with relatives while she would be away in Iowa City. The relatives with whom Rosemary, Coreen and I would be staying were mom's sisters and brothers, and only briefly with Dad's sisters and brothers. Many years later I would learn that there was considerable prayer and discussion on the part of Dad's sisters and brothers concerning our welfare. In retrospect, with a couple exceptions, Dad's family members were more loving, caring, and Christian than Mom's. How or why the decision was made that we would stay with members of mom's family remains unknown. However, I still cherish the times I was able to spend with grandpa and grandma, uncles and aunts and cousins on my Dad's side of the family, and other members of the Pedersen families.

When Mom and Dad arrived at the V.A. they learned that Dad was scheduled for surgery. All the pre-surgery steps were taken and he was prepped for surgery. The surgery was extensive. An incision was made beginning behind his right ear, down the side of his neck, and stopped in his right armpit below his right shoulder. Most, if not all, of the muscle and lymphatic tissue was removed from this large area. After some time he was released from the hospital, allowed to return home, and was to check with our doctor again as soon as possible.

— "Me and Daddy" —

— "Me and My Sister Rosemary" —

— "My Aunt Erma - Cousin Billy Lee & Uncle Bill Tordoff" —

"Coreen and Rosemary"    Coreen, Mom - Dad - Rosie & Me"

"Rosemary - Mom. Coreen - Me"

My Parents Harold & Arlene Pedersen on their Wedding Day March 17, 1940

"Me - Mommy - & Daddy"

My Maternal Grandparents
Clara & Ben Cassem

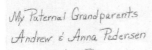

My Paternal Grandparents
Andrew & Anna Pedersen

Confirmation.

High School Graduation
1961

Graduation from
Mankato State College
1967

Judy - Dave
Wedding Day
"Our Wedding Day"
August 27, 1966

"My Wife Judy and I"

"Our Children - Angie, Sheila & Josh"

"My Daddy in Uniform" — "My Mommy"

"Me and My Daddy"

# Chapter 12
## My Anger Becomes an Attitude
## as I Defend Dad's Honor

After returning home following his cancer surgery at the Veteran's Hospital in Iowa City, Iowa Dad looked good, but I could tell that he appeared to be a little different and more tired. His calm disposition was still present, but his sense of humor didn't seem to be what it used to be. Anyway, it was great to have him back home. Naturally I felt everything would now be back to normal. Little did I know this was not to be the case.

When Dad saw our local doctor as he was instructed, he explained everything to him. He told Dad the biopsy specimen taken in Greenland had tested positive for cancer. His diagnosis was "Non Hodgkins Lymphoma." He also told Dad that because so much tissue was removed they were hopeful that all of the cancerous tissue was now gone. It was not the news he wanted to hear, but yet there was a ray of hope in what he had told him. Dad explained everything our doctor had told him to Mom, but the part about cancer was not yet told to us kids.

Dad reopened his shop, and it was almost as if he merely picked up where he had left off a little over a year ago. Word seemed to travel fast when it was heard the mechanic's mechanic was back in town! The only difference was that he seemed a little slower and not as able to withstand the long hours he was so accustomed to before the surgery. Furthermore, he still had not lost his touch. The quality of his work had not diminished one iota.

Life for us as a family now seemed pretty much back to normal, or so we thought. I even got my first bicycle. Boy, did I ever enjoy my bike! It was a brand new 24 inch Hiawatha. I had it all decked out with fancy handle bar grips plus streamers, a bell, a light, and I had even installed a speedometer. I could go as fast as 35 miles per hour downhill!

Because of the surgery, Dad's face sagged to one side, his right eyelid would not completely close, and the corner of his mouth seemed permanently hanging somewhat to the left in a downward droop. The huge long scar on the right side of his neck was very evident. Apparently during the surgery some nerves were severed resulting in this partial facial paralysis. Because so much tissue was removed from his neck and right arm, his right arm and shoulder were now considerably weaker, which I am sure was not only a blow to his physical body, but his mental psyche as well. After all, this man prior to the surgery, was a very well-built guy over six feet tall and resembled an NFL football player. Otherwise he seemed fine but somewhat subdued. Being a creative type of person, Dad made a small prosthesis to hold his lips and mouth in place. It consisted of a small piece of wire in the shape of a long "S" attached to a rubber band. One end of the "S" fit in the right corner of Dad's mouth, and the rubber band that looped over his right ear exerted enough tension to pull his mouth into a more normal position. It was a very ingenious and inconspicuous, simple and effective little device. Even though the prosthesis was not easily detected, it was still slightly visible; kids, one boy in particular, started making fun of Dad. They made jokes and rude comments about how weird he looked especially when he was wearing his little prosthesis. Kids would say how goofy or stupid Dad looked with that piece of wire sticking out of his mouth. This did not set very well with me and I ignored the nasty comments as long as I could. Then one day a boy named Mike made a malicious comment about Dad. That was all it took. He had lit my fuse and the fight was on. I don't recall the outcome of the fight, but I am pretty sure Dad's honor was not tarnished, and I made it very clear that Mike was making fun of my Dad and how he looked, and I was not going to take any more crap, or ignore any more bad comments from him or anybody else. From then on my fuse always seemed to burn a little faster. My mood, demeanor, and attitude also began to change. The chip on my shoulder became quite visible and I was not very shy about it being there.

The fight with Mike was just the beginning of future anger outbursts and resulting altercations that I felt necessary not only to defend my Dad's honor but also to pump up my damaged young psyche.

# Chapter 13
## My Deep Anger in Pre-teen Years Still was Not Recognized or Treated

It wasn't until I was in my pre-teenage years that I began to really show my woundedness; evidence which unfortunately went unrecognized. I began to display behaviors, actions, and say things totally inappropriate for a boy ten to twelve years of age. There was little or no help available to us through social services or counseling at that point in time. I became arrogant, argumentative, rebellious, disobedient, defiant, and cried a lot. I was often called the town crybaby! In my teenage years it became worse. I would become angry for no apparent reason. Many mornings I would wake up angry. I would have violent outbursts that often resulted in a physical fight with someone. I was verbally and sometimes physically abusive to my younger sister, Rosemary, for which I am now so very deeply sorry for displaying such fits of angry behavior. I think my behavior toward her had an adverse effect on her also later in life resulting in consequences from choices she felt were appropriate at the time, or were alternatives over which she felt she had no control; but ultimately were the result of adverse influences I may have had. As a result, she would make some poor decisions based on my inappropriate and abusive behavior. I was a very angry young man and seemed to be angry at everyone with no apparent reason or end. If Rosemary asked friends over they would ask, "Is David going to be there?" This type of behavior would carry over into my early adulthood when I was still displaying evidence that should have been recognized and dealt with but wasn't. It was not until many years later as an older adult that my mental and suicidal state would require the professional help of numerous doctors, psychiatrists, psychologists, counselors, hospitalizations, and medication. But that will be dealt with later in more detail. For now I will resume the ongoing angers of what I consider to be the cumulative episodes caused by the hammer.

# Chapter 14
## Dad's Serious Cancer Returns, Family Separated Third Time, More Trauma without Knowing Dad's Condition and Being Moved from One Relative to Another, I Recognize my own Anger

When Dad was younger he would occasionally experience migraine headaches. He started having severe headaches again. Thinking they were a recurrence of the migraines they were ignored at first, and Dad would suffer through them as best he could. As time went on the headaches became more and more severe and more frequent and would sometimes last for days. To get any relief from the headaches he would have to see the doctor, and be given a shot of some type of narcotic. We knew something must be wrong, but what was it?

After trips to various doctors proved fruitless it was decided he would return to the V.A. Hospital in Iowa City. Mom had Uncle Sammy drive and the three of them left for Iowa City in the Buick Roadmaster that Dad had rebuilt.

The lump on Dad's neck that was discovered two years earlier in Greenland had been determined to be cancerous. It was thought as a result of the extensive surgery he had previously undergone that any cancerous tissue had successfully been removed. Unfortunately that was not the case. The news was not good. The cancer had now spread to his brain. He would now have to undergo surgery once again.

Because Mom and Dad would probably be in Iowa City for a long undetermined time, as a family we were again separated for a third time without knowing Dad's condition. Being moved from one to another without an explanation was very traumatic. Each of us kids stayed with different relatives. At first I was to stay with Ray and Opal. Rosemary would stay with Aunt Lila and Coreen would stay with Aunt Bernice. I never knew the reason but on occasion we were moved to different relatives. Probably because we were either becoming a burden, and they were just tired of having us around, or maybe we did something wrong. The real reason for the mystical-musical-chair-relative-switcheroos was never clearly understood. The uncertainty of these moves added another dark layer to the box of unanswered questions lingering in my mind. Some of the relatives who had a cousin my age to play with were especially fun. Others without anyone I could play with or relate to were not so much fun, and as a result I would frequently get bored and into trouble with nothing to do. I always looked forward to spending time on the farms of my aunts and uncles, and I really enjoyed those who had me help with farm chores. The farming way of life really appealed to me. At one time I even thought about raising cattle out West.

An aunt and uncle were not very friendly, or even kind. I felt as though I was an inconvenience to them. It was as though I was a total stranger and not a family member. They had me sleep in a back storeroom on an army cot. It was a very lonely time and a sad time. We were not allowed to go visit Dad in the hospital so the only information we received with regard to his condition was in letters Mom would send us; or if someone happened to go to Iowa City to see Dad they may provide us with information regarding Dad's condition if they chose to do so. Not knowing what my Dad was going through caused me more fear and anxiety. We were going on nine months of uncertainty as to where we would be living and going to school.

There was no one who acknowledged my feelings or even seemed to understand what I—Harold's own son—was going through, or even seemed to care. The deep valley of serious things happening and my needs and feelings were not addressed as if a child like me was not aware

50

of emotions. Particular details about Dad's condition were withheld, poignant realities removed and my feelings and need to respond to him in some way were disregarded. I did not know if we were refused to see Dad because it was hospital policy, or because it was a five hour drive one way, and nobody was available to take us; or they just plain didn't want us to see him. In any case it was unfair, unkind, anxiety-producing and we were being deprived of seeing our Father at his point of greatest need. For me, serious dark and troubling things were happening emotionally and psychologically while my feelings were not being resolved. I harbored a considerable amount of anger over this issue for many years. I think it was more a case of stupid, esoteric hospital policy. Back then you had to be a certain age to be able to see patients in hospitals. Regardless of how hurtful the policy turned out to be that's the way it was. It may have also been that Dad's health had deteriorated to the point that it would have been too much of a shock for us to see him. Whatever the reason, it was not fair, and was causing me great emotional anguish over being helpless to get myself out of this awful predicament that I was in. I was definitely becoming a very angry young man!

# Chapter 15
## Silence Without Preparation to See Dad on his Death Bed as Sammy Drove Us 5 Hours to Iowa City

Finally nearly one year later we were told we were going to see Dad. It wasn't until much later I realized why we were suddenly permitted to see Dad when for months we were denied the opportunity. Rosemary, Coreen and I did not know that Dad was terminally ill, and they thought it would be a nice gesture for us to see him one last time before he died. Sometimes the best of intentions, regardless of the motive, turn out to be the most cruel. It was just more fuel to be added to my burning anger and despair. I was briefed before we left and was told that Dad was very sick and may not look the way I remembered him so many months before. I was also told to be very quiet, not to bother him very much, and that I would be able to stay only a few minutes. What a way to prepare a child for seeing his father alive for the very last time.

It was decades before the interstate system, so we had to leave very early in the morning in order to make the very long five hour trip to the V.A. Hospital. It was very quiet the entire trip with hardly any conversation. Normally adults seem to have something to talk about, even if it's the weather, the corn, or even gossip about somebody they know. Even Uncle Sammy, the family jokester, was almost silent the entire trip.

We finally arrived in Iowa City. Naturally having never been there before it all looked very strange. From the highway entering Iowa City, on the right at the top of a hill I could see the tall red-brick V.A. Hospital. Even today from the same vantage point of the highway the tall red-brick building still looks totally unchanged as it did some 60 plus years ago.

After Uncle Sammy parked our car we proceeded to the entrance of the hospital. The hospital, the lobby, the whole thing was huge. I thought the hotel in Mankato with the magic door was big; but this place was even bigger. After getting Dad's room number and directions from the registration desk we proceeded to find Dad's room.

# Chapter 16
## Absolute Shock Traumatized Me
## At 9 Years' old and Confirmed My Worst Fears
## Leaving Me Very Wounded Emotionally

What I had been told about Dad prior to leaving home in no way prepared me for what I saw as I entered Dad's room. The room had two hospital beds and both were occupied. The man in the farthest bed nearest the windows did not look familiar and I do not remember one thing about him. The first bed, the one closest to the door and the first one I saw upon entering the room was occupied by a man who looked vaguely familiar. Then I saw Mom sitting next to the bed. Was this my Dad? My eyes were riveted on my Dad as I stood there in total shock staring at what remained of a man that was supposed to be my Dad. The Dad I remembered was a tall man of about 6'1" or 6'2" muscular, but lean like a well-built athlete. This man was almost nothing but skin and bone and probably only weighed about 100 pounds. His face looked thin and drawn, and his wavy hair had been buzzed to a "butch" haircut. On the side of his head was a rather obvious large horseshoe shaped scar uncovered by hair; a tell-tale sign of a large surgical incision now healed over. He couldn't speak but he acknowledged our presence by looking and nodding at us. As he looked at me I sensed he was very ill-at-ease with me seeing him in his present condition, and as our eyes met my heart sank. I didn't know what to do. I didn't know if I should say anything so I just stood there in absolute shock. He also appeared to be in discomfort because he tried to change positions on his own but required assistance.

Mom tried to make him more comfortable, but as she did so he had this look on his face that I think was saying "I really thank you all for coming such a long way to see me and I appreciate it very much; I'm glad to have seen all of you. I don't want to be rude, but I think I would just like to be left alone right now." My worst fears are now true. Who will help me feel secure?

Not only did Mom look tired; she appeared to be exhausted and like Dad, she too appeared to have lost weight. With one exception, all these months Mom had spent every evening at his bedside.

I didn't know how to react. I felt like crying, but couldn't. I wanted to talk with Dad, but couldn't. My body felt like it wanted to stay, but also wanted to leave. I wanted to leave, but also wanted to stay. I felt paralyzed. I didn't know what to do or say for fear it would be the wrong thing to say or do. I was traumatized beyond crying. I was not given the time and attention to be able to feel and grasp what had happened and to comprehend the reality of this situation. Finally the decision was made to get something to eat so Pete could get some rest.

As we left the room I felt an uneasiness about leaving, but at the same time I felt an uneasy relief, and yet I didn't understand why my heart was racing and aching at the same time. What is happening to me?

We left to get something to eat and all the while the atmosphere was very somber. Even Uncle Sammy didn't have much to say. It almost seemed as though everyone knew something that Rosemary, Coreen and I didn't know, or weren't supposed to know, and they were not going to tell. Keeping the truth away from us added to my uncertainties. The whole atmosphere, attitude, and tenseness of the moment seemed impenetrable!

After we finished eating, Mom wanted to go to a store to get some personal things for herself and for Dad. I think it was a Ben Franklin Store. I had a couple dollars so I looked around while Mom got what she needed. The uneasiness I had experienced in Dad's hospital room still had not dissipated. I felt in control but also felt out of control. Why couldn't I get control? After paying for her items, Mom found me looking at a small model ship. Since I enjoyed assembling various kinds of models, I decided to spend my couple dollars and purchase the model ship. All of a sudden when I reached into my left pocket for my money and couldn't find it I burst into tears. The emotions of the day had apparently peaked and taken its toll and I could not hold back the tears any longer. Mom asked me what was wrong and in between sobs I withheld the real reason of my Dad's condition and said "I can't find my money!" The tears just would not stop. I was totally embarrassed as the clerk watched me frantically search for my money. Still sobbing, I checked my right pocket but nothing was there either. Mom then apologized to the clerk for the cumbersome situation. I again checked my left pocket and there was my money. Why I couldn't find my money in my left pocket the first time I do not know. I paid the clerk for the model kit and we left to return to the hospital.

We stayed longer at the hospital this time. It was still very difficult to see Dad this way. This was not supposed to happen. He was not supposed to be so sick like this. What was happening to my hero, my mountain mover, my anchor, my best friend? I didn't want to go home. It was now early evening when someone said we should start for home. We had another five hours on the road to return home. We told Dad goodbye but I don't think he heard us. Mom walked us to the entryway, and everyone went to the car except me. I started crying again and told Mom I didn't want to go. She did her best to comfort me but she needed comforting herself. Even though it was not a wise thing to do emotionally she kept telling me I was a big boy and needed to be strong for Rosemary and Coreen, and that she would be home as soon as she could. Between sobs I again told her I didn't want to go. She finally convinced me that I should go home. We stood there in the hospital entrance for quite some time just silent. Neither of us said anything for a long time while the rest were waiting for me in the car.

At that time I am pretty sure Mom knew Dad did not have much longer to live. I just didn't understand. She hugged me, kissed me, said she loved us very much and opened the door. With tears still in my eyes and dripping down on my cheeks I looked over my shoulder as I slowly walked to the car. Mom was still standing there waving goodbye. That day was the last day we saw our father alive. Another "Yah Ta Hey" moment and another hammer blow to my existing shock and grief that reopened my old wound of separation and seemed to be festering out of control.

# Chapter 17

## I Feel the Cold Sense of Loss, I am Immobilized by Loneliness, The Shop is Cold, and God Is Not There for Me at My Point of Deepest Need

It was Easter Sunday 1954, my sisters and I had been staying with different relatives. I was again staying with Ray and Opal. That afternoon we went to visit some of their friends. They had a boy Gary who was about my age. We played together all afternoon. Gary and I were too busy playing to hear what the grownups were talking about. At one point I thought I heard Gary's Dad ask something about a service; when it would be held. Since I didn't know what they were talking about I ignored what he had said. Finally Ray and Opal said it was time to go so Gary and I finished what we were doing and we left.

As soon as we got into the car and before he even started the engine Ray said, "David, we got a telephone call today, your Dad died today!" I started to cry and finally realized what they had been talking about earlier. This was a cold and insensitive way to tell a grieving young boy who was trying to understand the reality of his father's death. Now I remember Gary's Dad asking when the funeral would be. Now I understood why all of a sudden we were all allowed to see Dad. They all knew Dad was dying and didn't have much time left to live. Even though I was still in total shock it was all becoming clear to me now. It explained everyone's behavior and attitude and why everyone was being so secretive. I was extremely sad and overcome with grief. I felt angry and at the same time felt as though I had been betrayed. I felt so alone not even God seemed to be near.

We drove to our home above Dad's shop and walked in. The shop was totally void of any vehicles waiting their turn for Dad's magic. Dad was only 35 years old! Why? Being empty the shop was huge; I felt cold inside and still completely all alone. Dad's tools all hung neatly in their places and I became overwhelmed with the thought that his big hands would never touch them or me again. By now I had run out of tears even though I wanted to cry and never stop.

My life had just been suddenly shattered like a giant earthquake. Not only was my Daddy gone forever but my rock, my beacon, my mentor and best friend had just been stolen away from me like a thief in the night. What would I do? What was I supposed to do? What would become of me without my Daddy? What was now expected of me? What would I become? The dreams and future plans my Daddy and I had shared were now suddenly ripped away like a wild animal attacking its prey leaving only raw flesh exposed; with tears now completely depleted all I had left was the pain of loss and fear of uncertainty. It was now apparent that God, whom I had been taught as a child to love, trust, and, obey was not going to intervene as I thought and expected. There was only total silence and disbelief as I stood there all alone. The depth of the coldness that evening in Dad's empty shop was bone chilling. I don't think I have ever felt so cold and so alone. I tried to walk around the shop trying to feel some warmth and Dad's presence but none could be found. It was as if I was paralyzed. I could not move. I just stood there all alone with no one to comfort me. I felt numb, alone, scared and as if I was permanently adrift in a sea of uncertainty. God why did you abandon us at this hour of greatest need? We were true believers and yet you let us down. How do you expect us to be faithful to you now? Lord God, help me to understand.

As so aptly stated by my dear uncle Ruben.
In your sorrow:
Tenderly, may time help heal your sorrow
Gently, may friends ease your pain
Softly, may peace replace heartaches
     and may warm memories remain
     may you find assurance in His Word
     strength in His presence
     comfort in His mercy,
     and peace in His love.

Amen

## Chapter 18
## Mother Arlene Grief-Stricken, Sedated, Hospitalized, More Trauma, Sting and Pain of Sorrow, Fear, Loneliness

Dad's friend Red (Robert) who lived next to Dad's shop came over shortly after we arrived at our home, which was also the shop. Red, Ray, and Opal talked, but I heard nothing of the conversation and was not asked to take part in anything they were discussing. I later assumed they were probably discussing possible funeral arrangements, what would happen with the shop and equipment, and when my mother Arlene would be returning home. I just stood there frozen in time, trying to comprehend the depth of what I had just lost. Some people drove to Iowa City to get Mom and our car because she was in no condition to drive home five hours by herself. After days have gone by, Mom finally returned home.

Mom Arlene was so grief stricken that she was a basket case. I had never seen her like this before; she seemed to be someplace far off! I was feeling more loss and insecurity and wondering if my mother would be there for me. The day Dad died I think Mom basically also died. They loved each other very much and the two of them were meant for each other; they were soul mates. Before Dad died we were a normal, loving, Christian family and often demonstrated our love for each other; and also for others in need. But the day Dad died all that changed; our lives were now torn apart never again to be the same.

Oh! The sting and pain of sorrow cuts like a knife and leaves open raw wounds that seem to linger forever. Not only was I wounded but I also felt robbed and abandoned. I was robbed of my father and my childhood! Being a child of ten, my childhood as I knew it was suddenly and painfully taken away from me forever. I would never feel the secure and free feelings of a ten year old child, or an eleven year old child. Or, for that matter never feel what twelve, thirteen, or fourteen year olds would normally feel. It made me very angry and I did not understand that there was no safety net, no social service, no individual to help save me. It was troubling to me that even God seemed absent when I would cry out for help." What does Matthew 28: 20 mean when it says "Lo I am with you always?" Where were you God when I needed you most?

# Chapter 19

## My Anger and Confusion with Myself and God. In Retrospect I Think This Was the Beginning of My Clinical Depression

The time after my dad's death and during my teen years was a very confusing and trying time for me. I put down on paper the confusing and angry thoughts that I had because it illustrates the state of my mind and is part of my story. It is a common experience to direct anger toward God when there is nobody left to blame for our troubles just as I did.

Was I angry? You bet I was angry. What confused me is with whom am I angry? Is it God? I think some of my anger was toward God. Is it myself for not having enough faith? At times I felt so angry I would fantasize and play or act out how I would punish, or even get even. I would sometimes think of awful things I would do to get even. The weird thing is I could never identify who or what I felt this anger and punishment toward! Even after all these years it is still sometimes unclear. Even after 60 plus years I am still sometimes angry.

How do I get rid of these ill feelings? How do I rid myself of these feelings of anger after all these years? How do I rid myself of the feelings of wanting to punish or get even? Even if I could somehow miraculously get even would it change anything? At times I wish I could go back to being a nine, ten, eleven or twelve year old boy and experience what normal feelings and enjoyment would be like. With whom should I feel angry? Should I be angry with those who told me I was now the head of the family and would need to take on more responsibility and suck it up so to speak? Again at the time I believed them, and there too I harbor no grudge or ill feelings toward them. Also, what feelings am I supposed to be experiencing? Numbness comes to mind. I've already mentioned I felt confused. Do I feel sad? Yes, I'm sad at times. Do I worry? Yes, at times I do worry. Do I ever feel disappointed? Of course I have, but again I do not know with whom I should be disappointed. Have I ever felt scared? You bet! At times I have felt absolutely petrified. Have I experienced any other feelings? I probably have but at the present time I don't have a clue what they might be. I guess that brings me full circle back to confusion and with whom I am to be angry! The only one left is myself. To be so angry at myself is to add self-hatred to the emotional problems I already have. When that amount of anger and self-hatred is turned inward, as it was with me, it is a true definition of depression.

I am feeling more loss and insecurity. I think this is because our family began its dysfunctional downward spiral. When Mom returned home from Iowa City she was so hysterical with grief that she was taken to see our local doctor and eventually hospitalized. She had to be very heavily sedated and as a result was not even able to attend Dad's funeral. For that, my mother received some unfair, unkind, inappropriate criticism. How could she not attend her own husband's funeral? At the time, Mom was incapable of acknowledging that she would never be able to experience again the loving affection she and Dad had for one another.

As for me I was lost, angry, and felt permanently adrift in a fog. Not only had I lost my father, but also my best friend, my idol, and my mentor. There would be no more carburetor or fuel pump sessions, no more playing catch in the back yard, no more walking together in cornfields hunting pheasants, no more fishing together, no more showing me good places to set my traps. He would not see me play football, baseball, compete in track, graduate from high school, or any other part of my adult life. Emotions at times would eat at me like acid on metal.

When Dad got sick and died my safety net also was gone. It was unexplainable to me. Dad's death was too big and too much for my little brain and heart to take. It was no longer safe to be small, weak, dependent, and scared anymore. My only option was now to be strong. I could never be scared or show any weakness. Acting out and shutting down emotionally was much safer and that is exactly what I did.

In retrospect, I think my clinical depression was now beginning and would soon be on a fast track and speeding up at warp speed. I began to fantasize. I would think Dad was on some secret mission somewhere; and when he was finished he would return home. I would conjure up all kinds of excuses why he was gone; but each time in my fantasy he would return home to us, it would be as though he had never left and we would all live happily ever after. Fantasizing is a way of coping for a child and I became very good at it.

At this current time, I believe in the promise in Romans 8:14 that "all who are led by the Spirit of God...have received the spirit of sonship. When we cry 'Abba! Father!' it is the Spirit himself bearing witness with our spirit that we are children of God, and if children, then heirs, heirs of God and fellow heirs with Christ." Abba's best translation from Greek to English is "Daddy." For me and others who have lost our earthly fathers, I find this to be truly comforting because this promise gives me a real sense of belonging to God's family! Abba is my loving Heavenly Father, like a caring Daddy to His children. He has promised that He is feeling all the pain and anguish right along with us. When a burden is shared with 'Abba' one does not feel the full weight of the burden.

## Chapter 20
## My Input Was Not Included in Dad's Funeral Plans, Overlooking Was Disregard That Fueled More Lasting Anger

Prior to Dad's funeral there was considerable family discussion concerning how Dad's funeral should be conducted, what casket, and even how Dad should be positioned in the casket. Not once were we children asked for our input. It was as though we didn't exist. We probably would not have been much help anyway. One of Dad's brothers, a very outspoken uncle, who could be a very intimidating person, took it upon himself to take charge of Dad's funeral and essentially had everything done his way. Dad was missing the middle finger on one hand. Many years ago he accidentally nearly severed it while cutting meat and it had to be amputated. He had a deformed thumb on the other hand from an injury as a youngster cracking walnuts. Normally when a body is placed in a casket their hands are either folded or overlapped on the front of their body. Not Dad! Mr. In-charge said because of the missing finger and deformed thumb it wouldn't look right to have them visible. As if it would make any big difference. So he ordered to have Dad's arms straight along his sides with his hands out of sight. That's not all! Dad was a World War II veteran and entitled to full military honors. Well, Mr. In-charge decided that because he was not killed in action there would be no military funeral. Although, he did agree to a flag. Big deal! But at my age I was in no position to argue. Besides, my cousins and I were afraid of him anyway. There was no way I wanted to be on the receiving end of his wrath. On one occasion I had witnessed his anger and was not about to stir up that hornet nest again!

# Chapter 21
## Another Separation Brought About Rebellion Against God and Feeling Unattached

Again Rosemary, Coreen and I were separated. It seems nobody was concerned about keeping us together to regain some semblance of a family bond again. Mom was still under medical care, desperately trying to cope with losing the love of her life, and wondering how she could financially support three children. I was taken out of school and was sent to stay with Erma, Bill, and my cousin Billy Lee. I stayed with them for quite some time and went to school with Billy Lee. I don't know how Rosemary and Coreen felt. They were probably still too young; but by now I'm getting pretty used to the routine. I would stay with one relative and just about the time I began to feel any acceptance or comfortable being there, and before any familial bonding could begin to take place, or feeling like a member of the family; off I would go to another relative. After a number of these rotations I began to feel unattached, and unwanted like I didn't really belong anywhere. At the same time, I was also trying to keep my anger in check and my feelings of contempt under control as best I could for a young boy who now was expected to automatically conduct myself as an adult.

I think it was at this point my psyche began to feel really confused, and the only person I felt I needed to answer to was myself. I felt God had also turned his back on me. Why would God let such a thing happen to a happy loving Christian family? If God was going to be that way about it, I began to feel I didn't need Him either. I was now even rebelling against the very God who was to be my final source of comfort and strength. Where are you Lord when I cry out to you?

## MY POEM: REFLECTIONS

Seeing myself in retrospect as a ten year old boy
A light for my path is what I ask
Your gentle hand, Lord, to guide my daily task,
And if I should stumble and fall,
I know you heed each beckoning call.
It was Easter Sunday of 1954,
When my father was taken forever more,
"He's dead," I was told at eventide,
I gave in to the tears welling up inside,
Sobbing deeply I was held closely to Raymond's side.
What did I feel that fateful night
    now that our future seemed not so bright.
When told to be strong and bold,
All I knew, death felt very cold,
With tearful eyes asking God while so sad,
Why Lord did you take my Dad?
You say you are a great God loving and true,
Because of what you have allowed now I have only anger for you,
Not only did you take my father away,
You did not answer for healing when I knelt to pray.
How then God can you say trust and believe,
When sickness, pain. and sorrow you don't relieve.
My anger, God, boils over now for you
    as I tearfully wonder what to do.
Not only have you allowed me sorrow and grief,
You have now placed us all in total disbelief.
The things you have stolen from my life
    have cut deeply as a knife.

Not only have you broken my heart,
To now go on, I know not where to start.
Why Lord do you now place such a weight on me
When all I want is to set my sorrow, pain, and anger free.
This valley Lord, why can't you see,
Is lonely, dark, cold and oh so painful now for me.
My faith has now been shaken to the core
Lord take away our grief but faith restore
Make your answer, Lord, clear to me
I earnestly ask you, Lord, answer my plea.
What now should I think when much time has passed
The questions now – do they remain the same that I ask.
Regrets I must now admit
To these Lord help me to repent.
Your thoughts, Lord, I know are not the same as mine,
Yours, Lord, are higher and more divine,
Your ways, Lord, are what I questioned so in the past
I must now admit, Lord, your future is what will last.
If trusting more in you, oh Lord, is to be,
From my valleys, Lord, please set me free.
Your closeness, Lord, is what I long for,
Your grace I hope to cherish ever more.

**Author's Epilogue to Reflections**

How has God healed my wounded heart?

What I see, believe, and testify today compared to 68 years ago has been a journey of healing and spiritual growth! My battle with clinical depression has resulted in healing my wounded heart even though I still retain a huge scar which I cherish because it serves me as an ensign, a banner of God's love, a victory flag over emotions I could not control; it reassures me that God is Almighty, real, compassionate and is performing miracles even today. He knew my emotional and spiritual needs and right where He could perform His greatest healing and restoration to my desperation, loneliness and fear. This in turn caused me to humble myself before Him and resolve to more fully appreciate God's Grace, Redemption, and endless Power to make new. True freedom occurs by knowing, acknowledging, and accepting Christ as my guide on life's journey.

# Chapter 22
## Together Again as a Family is Painful, Confusing Dysfunction Evident

Now there even seems to be a pain of being together as a family. Being back together after all the separations seemed to increase my feelings of sadness, emptiness, loneliness and anxiety. Mom was gradually trying to come to grips with the death of her soul mate; while she continued to worry about finances. She never graduated from high school and had no marketable skills. She was a housewife and stay-at-home Mom. What was she to do? Since Dad was a veteran we were entitled to some financial assistance, but it was barely sufficient to provide for three children. Finally we were together as a family, or what was left of it, but it was not the same. I think each of us had changed somewhat from being separated and now we were suddenly thrust together again and that resulted in a pain of togetherness. What is this family togetherness thing we are now supposed to magically melt into with no instruction book?

Grief and loss were still very fresh in our minds, very tender, painful, and unrelenting. We were not trying to resolve our grief because we did not know how to deal with it. It was left to remain unresolved in our family system with each one of us trying to get through it in our own way. I think, in addition to grieving the loss of a husband and a father we were all very confused. The confusion continued to get worse.

I know I was confused. My behaviors were erratic. My emotions were all over the place. I was sometimes rude and inappropriate again, and sometimes just weird and off the wall. I would burst into tears for no reason and as a result was still labeled the town cry-baby! I was made fun of and mocked. One day I was called a "sissy" because I happened to wear a pair of reddish brown overboots to school because of the weather. They were just plain reddish brown rubber boots like the ones anybody could wear in bad weather or working in the garden. Just because they happened to be an exact copy of my mother's, I was humiliated one day at school when someone asked whose girl boots were in the boys' cloak room. I had to admit they were mine, and I was the only one who didn't think it was funny! Just another hammer to try to endure or escape!

Mom decided to put Dad's shop up for sale hoping it would sell right away. Unfortunately it did not sell right away. It finally did sell after a number of years, but there was still a mortgage on the shop. When it finally did sell and the balance of the mortgage paid off there was just enough to make a down payment on a house in town.

We moved from our apartment above the shop, and away from our acreage that was my comfort and my home, to a house in town that was located three blocks east of the school. It was not a fancy home but it had to do because it was all Mom could afford. Would our painful experiences now end?

# Chapter 23
## Vulnerable and Molested Leaving Me With An Unwanted Shameful Secret

Another painful incident took place that revealed my vulnerability and is still too sensitive to discuss even today. It is one that should have been reported to authorities. I think Mom suspected something and asked me about it. But, I was too ashamed and embarrassed to admit it so I lied and said "no." In fact I never told anyone until a few years ago when I happened to mention it to a therapist during one of my many therapy sessions. Even when she asked me if I wanted to discuss it again I said "no," and changed the subject.

One of my uncles had an elderly single hired man to help on the farm. I knew him because I spent a lot of my free time with my cousin on the farm. Sometime after Dad had passed away and we had moved to town, the hired man came to visit. He asked if I would like to ride along to visit a friend. Mom thought it was OK so I went along. On the way home after visiting his friend he suddenly stopped the car and sexually molested me in the car. I didn't know what to do. All I knew was that it was wrong. I wasn't about to tell anybody. I felt so ashamed, dirty, and cheap. If I did say anything and the word got out I would be humiliated again with some kind of new label in addition to the town cry-baby. Some days later a brand new fancy bicycle appeared. How was I going to explain this? Mom asked me again if he had done anything. I was still too ashamed so I lied again and said "no." Mom talked to Ray about it and Ray told her he was probably just a lonely person and since he had no family he just enjoyed giving gifts. That's the way it was left. I kept it a secret until the day I mentioned it to my therapist after it had haunted me for over 60 years. It is still a tender painful subject that I would rather it stay buried and never surface again. It is one of those ugly valleys that to this day still comes into view and occasionally wanders aimlessly through me not knowing how to escape.

# Chapter 24

## The Eleven Year Old 'Man of the House'
## is Overwhelmed by Expectations
## I Feel Helpless as I Try to Make Things Better

We were trying to recover from my father's death and my mother's hospitalization and I found it rather strange how people with the best of intentions would say things like "You're the man of the house now." All of a sudden I was supposed to be a 21 to 25 year old adult in an 11 year old body! "Your mother is going to need a lot of help now." "Make sure you give your mother all the help she needs now in her time of strife." "Take good care of your sisters." "You're a man now and they are depending on you!" "It's time to put your big boy pants on now." How absurd! That is a tremendous burden to place on a young boy. What was I supposed to do? What could I do? I tried to be a wage-earning adult when I went door-to-door selling garden seeds.

I had a paper route and mowed an occasional lawn. During the summer, my cousin and I occasionally hired out to farmers to help with their bailing and walked beans and corn. In the winter I had a trap line. What is it that was being asked of me? I felt helpless and overwhelmed when all these efforts to help and to be a man were not making things better. Our granddaughter is now eleven years old. It would be like asking her to do the same thing if her parents were suddenly gone. What a terrible responsibility to place on a child and rob her of the childhood she is entitled to enjoy; not to obligate her to some adult responsibility she would be incapable of handling at such a young age. It is inexcusable!

One thing definitely not asked of me, but one I slid into with Satan's help was assuming the missing male parental role. I seemed to slip into this role with reckless abandon. It turned out to be a total disaster. Instead of being the helpful loving son and sibling to help bind our fractured family closer together, I become just the opposite. I began to show less respect for my mother and would sometimes be verbally abusive to her. I would inappropriately try to discipline my sisters. In doing so I would be both verbally and physically abusive to Rosemary. We always seemed to be arguing or fighting over something that I thought according to my self- imposed standard was totally inappropriate. When in fact I was the inappropriate one. Unfortunately I really thought I was right and doing what I was supposed to do. After all, I was now the head of the household. All I accomplished was to drive us further apart. I'm convinced that the way I treated my sister Rosemary literally contributed to some of the wrong choices she would make later as an adult because that's what she knew and thought to be normal.

# Chapter 25
## Death of My Almost Five Year Old Sister Coreen Replays the Traumas and Dysfunctions in My Family and Leaves Me Feeling Emotionally Trapped

If things were bad then things were about to become worse. One weekend I took the bus to Minneapolis to see relatives and to attend a big outdoors sportsman show. It was fun seeing my cousins and aunt and uncle. The sportsman show was fine but I was expecting to learn some outdoor skills and maybe some new trapping techniques which didn't happen. When I returned home, Mom said Coreen had been sick and she had taken her to the doctor. He told Mom that Coreen had a head infection and would soon recover. She had a slight fever that persisted for days. As time went on the fever gradually got worse. Finally the fever got so high Coreen became delirious. She would reach her arms out to me wanting me to hold her. I didn't know what to do, or why I did it, but I would push her away. She would reach for me again and I would again push her away. Her fever became worse and she was burning up. As her fever rose she became weaker. She was finally taken to the hospital in Estherville. The next morning as I was getting ready for school the telephone rang. We were told that Coreen had died from complications of pneumonia and measles. I am not a physician but I feel that she was misdiagnosed. I think it was more like meningitis or encephalitis; but not being a doctor that is just my opinion. Regardless, the soon to be five year-old little Coreen; the loving, tender child along with her father are permanently gone by death. My sweet innocent little sister was really looking forward to going to Kindergarten that Fall, and was suddenly taken from us just like Dad.

It was a devastating blow and another valley in which to be emotionally and psychologically trapped. How could I have treated her the way I did? She was reaching out to her big brother when she needed me the most and I rejected her. What was I becoming? How could I reject a young affectionate child when she so desperately was asking for my loving comfort and attention? This valley has also haunted me for over 60 years. I can still see her reaching out to me.

Now Mom had to experience grief again while grieving Dad's death was still very fresh in her mind. This time it was her child. Parents are not supposed to bury their children. Why is this happening to us all over again? What in the world is going on?

Like before, Mom was so distraught with grief she could not function. Again she needed to be heavily medicated, again hospitalized, and was incapable of attending Coreen's funeral. This caused more grief for Mom to have to work through for a second time. Again not being able to attend Dad's or Coreen's funerals caused some consternation among some of the relatives. I guess they thought it was a cop-out and she should "suck-it-up" so to speak. How could someone be so cruel at a time when they should be comforting and understanding? It is true you can sometimes choose your friends but you cannot choose your relatives. The big question is what is happening to me emotionally? After 60 years of guilt and grief from Coreen's death, my therapist suggested that I write a letter to Coreen.

**Letter to Coreen After her Death**

Dear Little Sis,

Oh, how I do miss you! My heart aches still! You are in my thoughts daily. You were snatched from us at such a young age and now you are permanently almost five years old. I will always remember your innocent loving nature, and how you were so looking forward to starting Kindergarten. Life is definitely not fair. In a matter of a few years three-fifths of our family was gone to the ages, and death like a thief in the night prevailed leaving pain and oh so many questions.

I remember the night you were taken to the hospital in Estherville as though it was yesterday. That was the last time I saw you alive! No matter how hard I try to forget that night it is permanently etched in my memory and to reminisce is so painful even now.

I was so unkind to you that evening. You were reaching out to your big brother and I pushed you away. Why I did that I do not know. Even today when I think about that evening I feel so guilty and ashamed. Can you ever forgive me? Nevertheless you have been and will remain permanently reunited with Daddy and with Jesus the Comforter, Savior, and Protector.

As I reminisce those early years before moving to town, even though it is very difficult at times, I try to remember the good times when you, Rosemary, and I would play together. Remember that one winter with Mom's help we made a horse out of snow? I remember you and Rosemary in your snowsuits sitting on that horse.

Remember that fourth of July during the Cassem reunion when Uncle Orville dropped his cigarette in the box of fireworks? Boy, what chaos! To think about it today is quite comical; but back then it could have easily turned tragic.

I often fantasize what life may have been like without so much traumatic tragedy. But life is real and there are no would haves, could haves, or should haves.

You have always, and will continue to have, a special place in my heart.

As always, your loving big brother,

David

# Chapter 26
## Tough, Troubled and Out Of Control
## Haunts Me with Regrets

By now I am fourteen and almost out of control. I have become very defiant. I am an angry time bomb looking for a place to explode. One evening I stole a car and drove uptown to the roller skating rink. Some of my friends were there and we decided to take a joy ride. As I was backing away another friend, Jeff, came running out and jumped up on the fender of the car. Like an idiot, I didn't stop to let him off the car. Instead I proceeded down the street at a high rate of speed. Tom from the back seat yelled "Slam on the brakes!" I slammed on the brakes and Jeff fell in front of the car and was very seriously injured. He could have been killed. He spent weeks in the hospital undergoing surgeries and skin grafts. Unfortunately, he is now permanently scarred for life both physically and psychologically because of my stupidity. This is yet another deep dark valley for me to travel and to haunt me for years to come.

Fights were a common occurrence. Size didn't matter. If they lit my fuse the fight was on. I don't think I lost many if any fights, but I sure lost a lot of friends. It is nothing short of a miracle that I didn't self-destruct. I was intensely angry with God for taking my Dad and Coreen. Plus I was angry with the world and almost everything and everyone in it. People with good intentions would try to talk to me about the error of my ways. I would agree with them and turn around and continue to be a jerk. I went through the motions I think to make me look good. I attended church and Sunday school and was in Luther League and Boy Scouts, but I continued to be a troubled youth. What was my true self? I didn't feel like I had any identity.

I went out for football and I excelled at it. I found it to be a release for me. At least in football I could legitimately hit someone and get away with it. I could vent my anger on other people. I hated authority and pretty much vowed to do my own thing while not caring much if I hurt anyone or anything in the process. Being rather fast I started out as a right halfback. I was used primarily for short yardage. Because of my speed and aggression I could actually mow right over some of the opponents. Then for some reason after a change in coaching staff the new coach moved me to offensive right tackle. I hated that position but I figured the coach must know what he was doing. One day at football practice the coach placed me across from Earl, a teammate who weighed 100 pounds more than me and was a foot taller. Earl hit me so hard it felt like being hit by a freight train. Nobody had ever hit me like that before. I vowed never to be hit like that ever again. To this day I do not know if the coach did it intentionally, or by accident. From then on I was the freight train and I didn't care who or what got in my way. That position didn't last long and I was glad about that. I think the coach figured I needed to have a few of my rough edges knocked off so he moved me to offensive center and defensive linebacker and that's where I stayed. I tried to outdo Earl in football at every opportunity. Offensive center is a rough position to play, yet it is also where all the action starts. As an offensive center I took more than my share of thumps, bumps, bruises and hard knocks, but I dished it right back. I would block and hit just as hard as I could. As an offensive center and defensive linebacker I did very well. With my speed and toughness, being a defensive linebacker was where I was able to do the most damage. As a result of my performance, I was named second team all conference in football my senior year in high school. The coach told me I received the same number of votes as the player who was named to the first team; but because his team had beaten us for the conference championship he had to be named first team and I second team. After losing to that team, which happened to be my Senior year Homecoming Game, the coach said "If everyone had played like Pedersen things probably would have turned out differently." That boosted my self confidence and well being, but it also gave a big boost to my ego. Now I knew I could play with the big boys. Watch out, David the Goliath slayer is coming! My bad, inappropriate behaviors now seem to be on an almost even keel.

# Chapter 27
## Mom Arlene College Bound Makes Me Proud

One day Mom and her friend Jo were visiting and Mom happened to mention her concern about our current financial situation. We were barely able to manage expenses but not getting anywhere. It seemed we just existed on an endless treadmill that didn't want to stop.

Her friend said, "Arlene why don't you enroll in the junior college and become a teacher? That's what I am doing," she said, and mentioned that a person can get a teaching certificate with only two years of college. "But how can I do that? I don't even have a high school graduation diploma because I never graduated from high school." "Well," Jo asked "Why don't you come along with me next week and we will talk with the dean and see what he has to say." The next week Mom rode along with Jo. When Jo was finished with her classes the two went to talk with the dean. Jo explained Mom's situation and asked if there was any chance she could enroll in the teacher education program. He thought for a moment and then told Mom if she could pass a college entrance exam he would waive the high school graduation requirement. Late that afternoon Mom returned home with her arms full of books and she was grinning from ear to ear. She was now enrolled at Estherville Junior College! She was now a college student!

She had passed the college entrance examination with flying colors. Mom had taken the initiative to do something about our financial situation.

Mom took her studies very seriously. She studied long and hard and did very well. In spite of all the hardships she was able to maintain nearly a 4.0 grade average. She completed the two year teacher program and was able to get a teaching position right in town. She was now the new third grade teacher. She loved teaching and was one of those special people who possessed the gift of teaching. She could relate to any child and she could motivate her students to learn regardless of their abilities. She had no discipline problems with any of her students.

Even the toughest and most difficult students that other teachers complained about did well in Mom's class. They liked her, respected her, and did well in her class because she respected them and created an environment in which they were willing to learn. Being a student in her third grade class was like a child peering into a store front window for hours with her nose to the glass gazing intently at something so interesting and desirable that to wait outside seemed almost unbearable. Mom created that "nose-to-the-glass attitude and environment" for each and every student in her class. I remember one time Mom saying, "with patience and understanding you can relate to anyone." It took me decades to comprehend such a profound statement.

# Chapter 28
## Arlene's Auto Accident Turns into 2 Failed back Surgeries and Severe Pain

Nevertheless darkness is again hovering on the horizon. Apparently there are more deep dark valleys yet to be traveled. One day Mom was on her way home from Estherville. Suddenly some idiot attempted to pass her and a car behind her against oncoming traffic. In an effort to avoid a serious head-on collision she quickly slowed and tried to pull off the road to allow the idiot to pull back in the proper lane to keep him from hitting the oncoming car in a head-on collision. In doing so she was hit from behind when the car following her was unable to stop in time to avoid hitting her. At first she didn't think she was injured. But shortly thereafter she began experiencing severe back pain. It was later determined that the result of the impact had fractured some vertebrae in her back. She was told the only solution was surgery. The procedure was to take a piece of bone from her hip and graft it onto the fractured vertebrae to fuse them together. She chose to go to Northwestern Hospital in Minneapolis. She underwent the surgical procedure and the surgeon declared it a success and she should soon have relief from the severe backaches. Before she could be released from the hospital she somehow got staph infection which really prolonged the hospital stay. It took weeks to clear up the infection. She was finally released and returned home. The wait for relief from the back pain got longer and longer. Days turn into weeks. Weeks turn into months and months turn into years. There was no relief. She returned to Minneapolis for a check- up to find out why she was still having severe back pain. After the examination the doctor informed her that the surgical procedure had failed. She would have to undergo surgery a second time. This time following the surgery she was placed in a full body cast. It was the middle of the summer and back then we had no air conditioning. All we had was a small fan. With the summer heat and humidity the body cast I'm sure was almost unbearable. After months of being in that god-forsaken body cast she returned to Minneapolis. The cast was removed and again the surgeon assured her that the operation was a success and soon she should have relief from her back pain. As before, the wait became longer and longer and still there was no relief. Again the surgery failed.

Now with the second surgery also a failure, options are few. She could learn to live with the pain in hopes a miracle would eventually release her of her agony or try pain medication. The auto accident and two failed back surgeries had taken its toll. In addition to the pain, Mom was now partially disabled. She had difficulty walking any distance, standing and sitting for any length of time.

In addition to her condition, Mom now has a new worry. Her teaching position could be in jeopardy. Because she needed to take so many sick days she could lose her job. Pain medication was prescribed and seemed to alleviate some of the pain so for now she could finish out the school year. She continued with the pain medication and while on the medication she became able to function more normally. We began to notice that the need for the medication became more frequent. In addition to the episodes of pain she started to experience very severe leg cramps. These were not regular, typical run of the mill cramps. They were deep, debilitating, paralyzing cramps and they were not short lived. When the leg cramps occurred her only relief was to have the doctor give her a narcotic injection. Unfortunately the doctor was not available every time she needed another injection. So the doctor made arrangements for the medication and taught Rosemary (age 8) and me (age 16) how to administer the injections. We had to keep a record of the date, time of day, dosage amount of each injection and by whom the injection was given. The medication was a mixture of a narcotic and another prescription. If I happened to be gone, Rosemary would give Mom the injection. If Rosemary happened to be gone, I gave her the shot. The regimen seemed to be working well and Mom seemed to be doing quite well, and I was able to be away more often.

# Chapter 29
## Employed, Authority Figures Tell Me
## That I Am Not College Material, Cops Know
## My Mischief, I Am Falsely Accused by Neighbor

I was working after school or sport practice and on Saturdays for the man who bought Dad's shop. Instead of being Pedersen Motor Company it was now called Mike's Auto Body and Paint Shop. I was mostly given the grunt jobs and dirty work but I didn't mind since I was also learning a trade while hoping to be as good as my father at repairing cars. I had no intentions of going to college. We didn't have the money. Besides, my high school principal told me I was not college material; one uncle said I would never amount to anything; another one told me I would never be half as good as my father at doing much of anything. I believed them. Authority figures never should have mentioned such unfounded dire and powerful predictions of my future; especially to a young man who was emotionally stuck at the age of eleven and incapable of dealing with life at the present time. This was another hammer to add to the list of my dark valleys.

Because of my frequent brushes with the law and my behavior, I was always on the local cop's radar. As an example, one evening I had just returned home from work. I was fixing myself a sandwich and in walked Harry, the local cop. He didn't knock, he just walked right in and said, "you need to come with me." I asked if I could finish my sandwich and he said, "No! You need to come with me now." I had no idea what was going on or why he was there. I left my sandwich on the kitchen counter and we went to his squad car. He didn't tell me why he had come other than, "Pedersen, you are in big trouble this time!" We proceeded west out of town to meet the county sheriff half way between Armstrong and Estherville. En route he asked me about the tires I had stolen. I know it must have been impossible for him to believe me; but I was totally innocent. I knew nothing about any tires being stolen. Apparently a neighbor, I will call him Rick, had told him the two of us had stolen tires from one of the local gas stations and sold them in Jackson, Minnesota. He still did not believe me when I told him I knew nothing about any tires being stolen; and that Rick and I were not even very good friends. We met the sheriff and he questioned me over and over, and I told him I knew nothing about any stolen tires. It seemed as though I was wasting my breath because neither one would believe me. Finally, after lengthy questioning the sheriff said, "I'm going to release you in Harry's custody, but so help me if I find you are lying I will do everything I can to see that you go to prison." Wow! He was exceedingly angry! I was not worried for two reasons. I was a frequent flyer with Harry the Cop, and had become calloused and pretty much anti-authority, and I knew I had nothing to do with any tires being stolen. But, with my fame and notoriety that's the way it was back then! After questioning Rick further he admitted he had lied about the two of us stealing tires. As it turned out no tires were even stolen.

Mike eventually closed the shop, I think because of financial difficulties. Dad's shop under Mike's ownership failed, leaving me unemployed. I went to work for Art's Way Manufacturing as a sheet metal welder. During my sophomore year of high school I was convinced I had enough education and that I could make it on my own. I was fully prepared to turn in my books, tell the school to shove it, and walk away. I had had it with ridicule, unfounded accusations, and harassment. Fortunately my mother, being much wiser than myself, convinced me otherwise and I returned to school.

My junior year in high School I began to notice an attractive young lady who was a freshman. With my background and the record I had made for myself I didn't think I had much of a chance to get to know her or even like me; but I sure liked her. I rarely talked to her, or any other girls for that matter, and I didn't talk to many other people either. I was considered a stuck-up jerk by many of the other students. My first thought about what she would see in me, meant that I never considered asking her for a date. Her name was Elizabeth but everyone called her Betsy. I knew her cousin, Paula, quite well because we attended the same church. One day Paula said, "I know someone who really likes you and thinks you are neat." "Oh yah. Who is that?" "Betsy," she replied. I couldn't believe it. I was shocked. I began to talk to her more frequently and tried to spend more time with her. We only lived about a block apart so it was easy to just run over and chat. She was good for me and I felt very comfortable being with her, so different from being with other students, including other girls. I didn't associate with many other people, especially girls. Other people didn't seem to be interested in me so that was fine with me. But there was something different about Betsy. For some reason she had a real calming effect on me that I had never experienced before. Back then I was a very angry young man. I seemed to have this driving force to seek revenge against anything or anybody that had any hint of lighting my fuse. But not so with Betsy. At first it was just a friendly relationship between Betsy and me with no hint of romance. But gradually I began to feel there was more than just friendship, at least on my part. Our relationship continued for at least a couple years and during that time I knew in my heart that I was in love with her and thought she felt the same about me. I was still working at Art's Way and my dream was eventually for Betsy and me to get married. I would continue to work at Art's Way since I wasn't going to college, and we would settle there in Armstrong for the rest of our lives. I was definitely in love with Betsy and frequently told her I loved her. It's funny how dreams sometimes seem to take on a life of their own completely devoid of reality.

# Chapter 30
## Another Valley of Loss of Love, Dream of Marriage Heartbreak, Separation, Rejection

I asked Betsy if she would marry me. I was not prepared for her reply. She said "No!" I was shocked beyond belief, hurt, and devastated. I couldn't breathe. Her response cut like a knife. It was one more separation from someone I loved. It was as if my life was a chess game and I was constantly in a defensive mode trying to avoid the inevitable checkmate; the ever present loser. I could not believe it. What in the world had gone wrong; or what had I done to cause her to reply that way? I thought she felt the same about me as I did about her and I did not want to lose her and would do anything for this not to happen. I would have done anything for her. But it was not to happen. After that we kind of drifted apart. I was still in love with her but didn't feel I could compete with the guy she was now seeing. That really hurt knowing I was in love with her and she was seeing someone else. The guy she was now seeing, who once was a best friend, was the one I slugged in the face with Betsy present one night after an altercation following a football game. Just another example of my uncontrollable rage and anger.

I tried to be a financial support to our family by working as a mechanic's assistant at the local car dealership and putting in very long hours at Art's Way. Playing in the band was a release; it was fun and we did some performing at various locations. One Summer we even played background music for a carnival side show. One of the acts in the carnival sideshow was a trained chimpanzee. He could do certain tricks and one of them was riding around in a circle on a scooter. I should have realized something wasn't quite right when each time the chimp completed a lap he would come a little closer to our rock and roll band. On the last lap he reached out, grabbed my arm, pulled the sleeve off my jacket and I almost dropped my guitar. We cancelled the rest of our engagements with that carnival. I'm beginning to wonder if there is anything I can do right!

I would continue to occasionally get into trouble with the law, but consequences for my actions really did not matter that much to me anymore. My destiny seemed pretty much set in stone. I would continue in the same old rut and any dreams or aspirations I may have had in the past, or even in the present, now seemed like long lost memories that would never materialize. Rolling with the flow and dealing with failures was now the name of the game and I was trying to figure out how to be content with my destiny. I had failed at becoming an auto body repairman when Mike closed the shop. I failed at Art's Way when I got laid off. I failed at a romance which I thought was a sure thing but only further broke an already broken heart. I no longer had a girlfriend and the only other outlet was to continue playing my guitar and singing in a small rock and roll band.

# Chapter 31
## Mom Arlene's Health Challenges Worsen, Hospitalizations, More Stress for Me, My Teenage Sister Rosemary and I Provide Care for Arlene

Mom was beginning to need more medical assistance. The injection medication was no longer as effective as it once was. She was needing the injections more often and I think she was beginning to lose her coping skills and hope to get better as well.

Tension was beginning to brew among some of Mom's family. One sister would borrow something and never return it. We had an extra washing machine that wasn't being used. One day she came over and took it home and when it was worn out and needed to be repaired she brought it back. One brother-in-law called her a drug addict and others just seemed to ignore us with the exception of one sister, Erma. Even though Erma lived some 30 plus miles away she would occasionally come to help with what needed to be done at the time. She was the only one who really seemed to care. Mom's brother who farmed north of town, seemed to purposely avoid us as though we were a burden to his agenda. There also seemed to be an uneasy feeling between Mom and Dad's family, the Pedersen's, which I didn't and still do not understand. Although I'm sure it was unfounded, Mom would occasionally make a comment suggesting this tension was true, which at the time probably should have been a red flag of concern. The Pedersen's were good Christian people so it was difficult to believe there were any ill feelings or animosity toward Mom on their part.

One of Dad's brothers was an ordained pastor and a missionary in Africa. Another was a traveling evangelist spreading God's Word of Salvation all over the Midwest and Canada. It just didn't seem possible. As a youngster I had spent considerable time with my Pedersen cousins and I saw no evidence of ill feelings toward Mom. I heard an occasional comment that could probably be taken as negative feelings toward some family members on Mom's side, but never about Mom. Still Mom would say she no longer felt comfortable or part of the Pedersen family after Dad died. I would learn many years later there was considerable prayer and discussion regarding the welfare of my sisters and me; and the possibility of who might be the best fit to take care of us since Mom's ability seemed to be waning.

In retrospect, I think that the overload of family stress was the beginning of what many people would refer to as a nervous breakdown. Mom's coping skills were beginning to decline. She had every reason to lose the grip on her coping skills, and to become somewhat emotionally unstable. Her calm nature and even disposition were disrupted by some erratic behaviors and occasional sudden outbursts of anger totally out of character for her and obviously suggested something was wrong. She was hospitalized under the care of a psychiatrist. When we would visit her she seemed perfectly normal, but reserved, tired, and yet somewhat comfortable which seemed to us to be typical of someone under the influence of medication. After being released from the hospital and returning home after some time the cycle would repeat itself; the ensuing emotional roller coaster appeared to be out of control, and we would make the return trip to the hospital. Not once did any doctor ever take the time to talk to Rosemary and me about any diagnosis or treatment plan for Mom; and no family members ever made the effort to visit her during her many hospitalizations which only fueled my anger.

# Chapter 32
## I Am Almost a 3.0 College Student, Life Held Back to Provide for Mom and Rosemary, Back in the Old Rut at Art's Way, Relationship with Pedersen Grandparents Blossoms

With no personal goals of my own, I just kind of rolled with the flow, but my demeanor and emotional state were still the same. I was still an angry, belligerent, arrogant young man. I don't know how Mom could put up with the likes of me. Mom must have had to make numerous sacrifices to be able to pay for her two years of college. Since I was already helping to support our family I knew the money just was not there.

A friend of my Dad's began showing up. He did a lot of good things for us and seemed genuinely happy to do them. Even though they were probably unnecessary they were still very much appreciated. I think his real reason for being there had to do with my mother. I think he was hoping he could kindle a romantic relationship with Mom. She eventually told him she was not interested, but he kept coming anyway and helping out just like he was part of the family.

One day he shocked me with a question. He asked me if I had ever considered going to college. I told him "no" because my high school principal had told me I was not college material, and we had no money for anything like that. He said, "If I pay your tuition would you go?" How was I to respond to such an offer as this? If I accepted his offer I would be leaving home, and that meant more responsibility would be placed on my younger sister, Rosemary, to help Mom. If I declined his generous offer I would just remain in the rut I was already in. I didn't know what to say. Was he really genuinely interested in my welfare enough to help me go to college, or was he trying to get me temporarily out of the picture thinking if I was gone he would have a better chance of wooing my mother? I thought he was becoming somewhat of a pest, and I was getting a little tired of him showing up all the time as though he had the right to be there. Betsy had turned down my marriage proposal so I knew there wasn't much future for me in Armstrong. I thought "it's his money" what do I have to lose. If I flunk out of college it will not have cost me anything, and I can just return to the familiar confines of my self-made rut! With some fear and trepidation I decided to take him up on his offer. If I flunk out I flunk out, but I would like to have the chance to prove to some people that I could do it!

I enrolled at Mankato State the Fall of 1963 and became a college student. As a Freshman in college I had no goals nor any college major to declare so the first two years I concentrated on the basic required courses. I discovered I actually liked college life, and actually did better in college than I had done in high school with almost a three point grade average; and I'm not supposed to be college material!

At first, I felt a little apprehensive about leaving Mom and Rosemary alone. Even though Mom was now doing much better I was still concerned. Would Rosemary be able to continue handling things on her own if something happened? So far everything seemed to be fine. Mom was up and around and functioning quite well. The medication injection routine was working when she needed it, but surprisingly she did not need it as frequently as before. That was good news. But then one day, while at college, I received word that Mom had again been hospitalized. This kind of scenario would repeat itself many times in the ensuing months. After each hospital stay we would take her home and we tried to do what we thought was best. During my second year of college, I dropped out to return home and work at Art's Way to help provide for Rosemary and Mom. Life wasn't great, but we were getting by and doing the best we could.

I began spending more time in Fairmont with my Dad's folks, Grandpa and Grandma Pedersen. They were very devout Christians and Grandma would always say we must pray for the grandchildren. Grandma would always have fresh homemade bread and cookies. Her home-made dark bread was exceptionally delicious, and one could expect such good food to be served at every visit.

Between my two grandparents they always seemed to have good advice. If I had a question they always seemed to have the right answer. If I had a problem they always seemed to have a solution. Grandpa filled in and became the father I had lost and Grandma became a second Mom. I still cherish the memory of that relationship. I miss them as much as I miss my father and little sister.

Mom seemed to be doing much better so after dropping out of Mankato State that one term I returned the next term, and tried to resume where I had left off. I was soon back in the groove so to speak as a college student, but college life was not the same. I was still trying to get over Betsy, my study habits faltered, and I almost flunked out that term. It was now Spring and the Summer terms would soon begin; but Mother Nature intervened. Mankato was experiencing a terrible flood. As a result, one could not get in or out of Mankato without permission and all classes were canceled. The college campus was completely shut down. I could have stayed like many other college students to help sand bagging efforts to control the flooding, but I felt I should take this opportunity to return home, and went back to work at Art's Way. It didn't take long and I was back in my old rut working and trying to stay one step ahead of the sheriff!

# Chapter 33
## New Relationship With Judy. Proposal Accepted. Married Life Begins

One weekend I went to visit my Aunt Erma, Uncle Bill, and my Cousin Billy Lee. While I was there I happened to meet a young lady who was renting a room from them. She worked for the telephone company as a telephone operator. The telephone office was not very far up the street so it was convenient for her to walk to work. We were introduced, exchanged pleasantries, and that was all that was said. I did notice something though. I don't know what it was exactly, but occasionally the way she either held her head, or maybe a facial expression that somehow reminded me of Betsy. I don't remember who it was, perhaps Mom, encouraged me to go see this young lady named Judy who was staying with Aunt Erma and Uncle Bill. I was still trying to get over the rejection from Betsy so I was not interested in any relationship at this point. I had already failed at one relationship so was not eager to plunge into another one for fear it too would fail. I was just trying to survive being back in college, going home on weekends to help out, and working part-time. Things were a little stressful to say the least.

I think there was some plotting going on between Aunt Erma and my mother. I think they were doing a little match making via the telephone, pun intended! One day Mom said, out of the blue, "Why don't we drive down to Erma and Bill's and you can see if that girl who is staying with them would like to go to a movie if she doesn't have to work?" I think they already knew she had the night off. So I agreed and when we arrived, low and behold, she was there, and yes it was determined she did indeed have the night off. Since

Billy Lee wasn't there I didn't have anything else to do so I asked her if she wanted to go to the show. She said she would and we went to the movie.

I found out she was fun to be with, attractive, and we had a lot in common. Her father had been a mechanic and died of cancer like my father. She enjoyed some of the same things I did. Our birthdates were in different months but only one day apart. Hers was on the 25th and mine the 24th. Before the evening was over I became very fond of this young lady named Judy. Our relationship soon blossomed and we continued to see each other when I could get away. After about a year, one evening when I knew Judy was working, I drove down and had Aunt Erma go with me and help pick out an engagement ring. Shortly before she was to get off work I drove up to the telephone office and waited to give her a ride back to Erma and Bill's house. When she came out she was surprised to see me waiting in the car. When she got into the car she was even more surprised when I gave her the engagement ring. She said "yes!" I was so afraid she would say "no" just like Betsy had done.

On August 27, 1966 we were married in the Congregational Church which was her home church in Humboldt, Iowa. Mom had been feeling better and doing very well. She looked like her old self and very stunning in the brown dress she had purchased special for the wedding. For our honeymoon, Judy and I went to the Wisconsin Dells. We had a great time.

I was in my Junior year of college so Judy and I moved to Minnesota. Our first apartment was a basement apartment located at 919 Range, North Mankato, Minnesota. North Mankato was a separate little town adjacent to Mankato. I guess you could call it a suburb of Mankato. I worked full-time at Kato Body Shop when I was not in class, and Judy worked at Sheri Candies.

A Pedersen cousin of mine lived in Mankato with her family. She invited Judy and me to attend church with them one Sunday. The church was not a Lutheran Church as I had been accustomed to back home. The music was good and the pastor had a good message. Even though it was not Lutheran I felt very comfortable there. After the service my cousin introduced us to the pastor and we went back to our apartment.

One evening there was a knock on our door. I think it was Judy who opened the door and there stood the pastor we had been introduced to the Sunday before. We talked and he would ask some of the usual questions one would ask when trying to get to know someone like what I was majoring in, questions about family, and various other related questions. Then he asked us that one big question. "If you were to die this evening are you sure you would go to heaven?" I had never been asked that question before. I thought I had taken my Lutheran Confirmation seriously, but this was a question for which I did not have a good answer. I think I fumbled with a reply like, "I guess heaven, but I don't know for sure." He then said, "Would you like to know for sure?" We replied with a kind of weak "yes." So the three of us knelt there on the floor next to the couch and Judy and I gave our lives to Christ. We chatted some more, he gave us some literature and left.

# Chapter 34

## Mom's Excruciating Pain Out of Control. No Help from Anyone Anywhere Leads to Hopelessness and Wit's End for My Sister Rosemary and Me During Her Teenage Years

Mom's health deteriorated even more. She was in pain more frequently and the pain medication had to be given more frequently than before. Poor Rosemary, barely a teenager, was trying to keep things under control at home. She would frequently call me and ask what to do. I was already driving home on weekends, but many times I would have to drive down during the week. We were still not getting any help from the local relatives. It was as though we didn't exist. It was a very stressful situation for everyone. I even wrote a letter to the doctor informing him of what was going on. I'm sure he already knew because in Armstrong, being such a small town, everybody knows everything about everyone almost at the speed of light. I even asked if there was anything that could be done that we were not already doing. I never received a reply nor any acknowledgement of receiving the letter. It annoyed me greatly and I felt disregarded. I thought I at least deserved an acknowledgement that he had received my letter. I felt completely abandoned, and I think Rosemary felt the same. We were left to our own devices. The injections for pain were still working somewhat, but were not doing anything for the severe leg cramps. They were so severe they would almost wrap her up in a ball, and she would just moan in agony. We tried heat, ice, massaging but nothing seemed to work. Eventually, probably out of sheer exhaustion she would doze off. It was awful to see her like that and not be able to do anything for her to relieve such pain and discomfort. She did not deserve this and it didn't end.

Unrelenting pain that never got better went on for another 11 months. Rosemary and I were at wit's end. Everything we tried was not working. Once, when we did take her back to the hospital they would not even admit her. They were even reluctant to see her. We considered again and again taking her back to the hospital, but when we once tried taking her for a ride in the car she got car sick. We considered flying her to the hospital. Ray said if she gets sick in a car she would surely get sick in an airplane. I felt so helpless and so guilty.

On July 20, 1967 the telephone rang. Judy answered the phone. She said "It's Ray" and handed me the phone. I said "Hello," and Ray said, "Your mother just died!" In shock I just stood there speechless. Finally Ray said, "David, are you there, did you hear me?" Still in shock I finally said I did and told Ray we would leave immediately. That was the longest 75 miles I have ever driven!

Apparently sometime during the night Mom finally had reached her limit. With hope totally gone, no longer able to cope, and wracked in pain; either by accident or deliberately to finally end her suffering, she overdosed on medication and quietly slipped into eternity. She was now free from pain, sorrow, and all her suffering. She would now be forever reunited with Dad, Coreen, and our loving Savior Jesus the Christ. What a glorious and welcome meeting that must have been!

Mom wore, one final time, that pretty brown dress she wore at our wedding. She wore it at her funeral and looked just as stunning as she did before. She was finally at peace and laid to rest next to her loving husband and her daughter who was now permanently almost 5 years old; both of whom she had grieved for so many years. Mom's funeral was not even normal if a funeral can be normal. The pastor of her church was out of town on vacation and was too far away to come back for her funeral. Since no local pastor was available a pastor from another town we didn't even know was recruited to conduct Mom's funeral service. I don't remember the pastor's name. I don't even remember anything of his message. Everything was so impersonal and lacking in comfort for the family. The only thing that made a family connection to our grieving hearts was Mom's favorite Bible verses in Psalm 121; that gave her comfort when her husband was in Greenland.

> I lift my eyes to the hills.
> From whence does my help come?
> My help comes from the LORD,
> > who made heaven and earth.
> He will not let your foot be moved,
> > he who keeps you will not slumber.
> Behold, he who keeps Israel
> > will neither slumber nor sleep.
> The LORD is your keeper;
> The LORD is your shade on your right hand.
> The sun shall not smite you by day,
> > nor the moon by night.
> The LORD will keep you from all evil;
> > he will keep your life.
> The LORD will keep your going out and your
> > coming in from this time forth and for evermore.

Even though the church was full it was still a very cold atmosphere. Even in death, Mom was cheated out of the dignity of having her own pastor. Why is it that at times of real need life sometimes has to be so cruel? Another final good-bye; a "Yah Ta Hey" moment. Another deep valley of grief ahead.

# Chapter 35
## Judy and I Start Our New Family
## While The Hammers Continue

September 1, 1967 Judy gave birth to our first child, a daughter Angela Marie. She weighed 6 pounds and 13 ounces. We were proud of our new little girl and happy to be starting a family of our own. I was also sad that Mom and Dad never got to see their first grandchild and Coreen never got to see her first niece. It wasn't meant to be. This just was not fair. In a matter of just a few years three fifths of my family was gone, taken away. God, where are you when we need you?

In December of 1967 I graduated from Mankato State. I should have graduated in the Spring; but because of dropping out for a time during my second year it took me longer to finish. I took a position as Speech Clinician and Hearing consultant with Hancock County Schools located in Garner, Iowa. Ray and Opal had since been appointed guardian of Rosemary and she lived with them so she could finish high school in Armstrong. Garner wasn't that far away so we could still be somewhat connected.

The valleys and the hammers continued. Shortly after I began working in Garner the County Superintendent called me into his office. He said, "Oh, by the way this position requires a Masters degree. You will have to begin working on a Masters degree in order to keep your certification and your position here at Hancock County Schools." Great! I just graduated a month ago with a BS degree and now I'm told I have to begin graduate work! I'm married, we have a five month old infant, a younger sister that also needs my support, and my mother just passed away a few months ago. What's the deal? Had I been told a Masters degree would be required at the time of my interview? No! Had I been told I could have applied for my certification prior to the deadline; and I would have been officially certificated by the time I began work, and would have automatically been grandfathered in with the understanding that graduate work and an advanced degree could be pursed at my convenience. He was aware of the new degree requirement; he just didn't tell me. I think he was more concerned about making himself look good with the County Board of Supervisors by not having any staff vacancies. He didn't care what we had recently been through, or what we would have to experience just to keep my certification and my job. My anger seemingly that had been under control was now beginning to surface once again.

I had a family to support so there was no way to enroll full-time into a graduate program and still keep my job. That meant I would have to find a program at a college or university that would allow part-time students. To make matters worse graduate level programs in Speech Pathology and Audiology were quite limited, especially Audiology, which was the field I was most interested in because it was a relatively new paramedical field; and therefore was even further limited. There were no such programs in the state of Iowa that accepted part-time students. That meant I had to look elsewhere out of state. I checked with colleges and universities in surrounding states and there were none. The closest one I found was Colorado State University in Fort Collins, Colorado. Then somehow I came across a brochure from the University of Wyoming. They were advertising a new graduate program in Audiology. As an incentive they would waive the non-resident tuition. That meant I could enroll for their summer terms, my tuition would be the same as for Wyoming residents, and I could still be back in Garner when school resumed in the Fall. But, what about Judy and Angela if they stayed in Garner? Where would I stay? How would I get there? If I drove Judy would have no transportation. If I didn't drive I would have no transportation. We only had one car. We found out there was married student housing available so Judy and I decided we could probably make it work if we went as a family. So for four years the first week of June after school was out in Garner we packed up everything and moved to Laramie, Wyoming. After the summer terms were done we packed up everything again and moved back to Garner. We did that arduous task for four years. Finally in August 1971, the guy who was not college material graduated with a Masters Degree in Audiology. I was the first one to go through their new graduate program in Audiology.

It was not easy. In addition to the rigorous graduate studies; I was still trying to deal with my past, the deaths of my father, little sister, and most recently my mother. It was taking its toll. The burden was getting to be too much and the valleys were getting deeper and closer together. At times, I felt life was unbearable; and at times I was probably intolerable to others as well, including my wife Judy. I think at one point, even though she never said so, Judy may have thought our marriage may have been a mistake and was coming to an end. One weekend, while in Wyoming, I took a break from studying and being in one of my many grouchy, unruly, unkind, and just plain being a jerk kind of mood, we drove out to a familiar picnic and camping area not too far from Laramie. As we were climbing among the rocks Judy said, "What's wrong, David, do you want a divorce?" I hesitated and finally said, "I don't know what's wrong, and as for a divorce, no I don't think so." What I did know was I felt lower than a snake's belly in a rut for no apparent reason with no way of escape. Fortunately she loved me enough, was patient enough, committed enough, and understanding enough that we were able to escape that valley and withstand the impact of that hammer to await yet unknown future valleys, challenges and life wrenching difficult situations and decisions; at least for the moment.

# Chapter 36
## Following the Deaths of My Father, Mother, Sister; Judy 's Life is in Jeopardy. We Had Twins-One Live Birth. One Stillborn Birth.

We were not free from valleys and hammers yet, however! On November 22, 1971 our second daughter, Sheila, was born. Early in Judy's pregnancy the doctor said he heard two heart beats. That meant we might be having twins. Late in her pregnancy, during another routine exam, the doctor said he heard only one heart beat and reasoned that the earlier second heart beat had been just an echo. A couple weeks after Sheila was born our neighbor and I decided one weekend to go to southern Iowa to hunt pheasants and quail. While we were gone Judy started to get sick, and when I returned home she definitely was not feeling well. A couple days later, while I was at one of my schools I was told I had a telephone call. It was our office secretary telling me I should come home immediately. Judy was hemorrhaging and needed to be seen by a doctor right away. I got her to the hospital just in time. Judy was really sick and bleeding profusely. It was determined that she was trying to deliver Sheila's stillborn underdeveloped twin. The doctor was correct when earlier he had heard two heart beats. What had gone wrong? Are you toying with us God? Another separation and loss for me to grieve. "God! these valleys are getting to be more than I can handle." For reasons we will never know, when Sheila was born, the doctors and nurses were unaware there was a stillborn twin inside Judy's body that was trying to abort itself. Instead of two babies together in one amniotic sac; apparently Judy was carrying two separate babies in two separate amniotic sacs during one pregnancy. During Judy's pregnancy only one thrived leaving the other one to perish in the uterus. That is the explanation why two heartbeats were heard early on and then eventually only one heartbeat. Judy, at this point, was extremely sick. She was losing so much blood I thought I might lose her too. Was I going to have to plan my wife's funeral? What do you tell your four year old daughter she no longer has a mother? I did not think I could withstand another loss of the love of my life. Again, God where are you? Besides, what does a young single father do, especially with two children, including a newborn infant?

I never told anyone, not even Judy. That valley haunted me for years, and to this day when I think about that day I still feel sad. Another innocent life lost. Another lost child. What would that person have been like? If the stillborn twin would have been anything like Sheila, they definitely would have been a hand full. Fortunately Judy recovered; but because of this recent trauma, and four subsequent miscarriages that followed; there was a strong possibility that there would be no more children. I now have somewhat of an idea how Mom felt when Coreen died even though circumstances were not the same; I still mourn the loss of both children. Life had been unfair and continued to be unfair.

# Chapter 37
## Trying To Move Forward While Straining Under the Valley of Financial Debt and Unresolved Anger Hammers of the Past

After five years we left Garner. Even though I was apprehensive about moving further away from my sister Rosemary, we moved to Burlington, Iowa. It was a good career move, even though it was not an easy move to make. In addition to not wanting to move further away from my sister, I certainly did not want to move southeast to Burlington. If I was to move, I wanted to move West.

I accepted the position as Educational Audiologist for schools in one county, and part of a second county. My responsibility was to develop, implement, and improve a somewhat already existing program; and to identify, evaluate and provide the necessary services to hearing impaired students in the area. It was a daunting task, but as my father had instilled in me with the carburetors and fuel pumps, I was never one to shy away from a challenge, and it certainly required full use of my very best abilities, energy, and knowledge. The first thing I learned after arriving was that even though I was the Audiologist, there was no existing Audiology program. All I had at my disposal were a few outdated portable audiometers. They were serviced and calibrated annually so they were still useable even though they were obsolete, and needed to be replaced. I also had no budget so there was no money with which to purchase anything. I was at the mercy of an administrator who probably still had the first nickel he ever owned, and had squeezed it so hard the Indian and the buffalo were on the same side.

The next thing I learned was that politics not only exist in government, but also in our public educational systems. Starting out with no funds, I decided that writing a grant would move the program toward allocation of federal and/or state funding so that we could obtain the necessary equipment required for the implementation of the Educational Audiology program for which I was hired. With considerable help from my supervisor a grant proposal was developed, written, and submitted to the Department of Public Instruction. In the process of developing the grant proposal I met with school administrators, teachers, and other staff members not only to inform them of what we were planning to do; but also to get their input, blessings, cooperation, and some ownership in the program. I was not prepared for some of what was to come. Countless times I had to virtually go through the proposal line by line, sentence by sentence, and defend practically every word to justify at length what had been written. It was ridiculous. There would be no cost to any of them. None of their sacred jobs would be jeopardized. It was a service to their students and children free of charge. But many felt so threatened by the word "change, or perceived change" that I began to feel like I was in a courtroom being cross-examined and grilled by a Philadelphia lawyer!

Fortunately the grant was approved. I had written the grant to be funded for only one year. The State Department thought it was such a good idea they funded it for two years. With the funds we were able to construct a room for testing and consulting, and equip it with a sound treated test booth and diagnostic equipment. We were also able to purchase special tests, materials, print brochures, and train certain individuals for specific tasks.

The program was a complete success. We were now able to actually evaluate students and children. We could actually do diagnostic hearing tests, make medical referrals when indicated, evaluate students for use of amplification, and actually help determine an educational plan of action for hearing impaired students and children in our area. Prior to the project all that could be done was screening, a basic hearing test and refer students to the University of Iowa for evaluation. When this happened the children we had to refer to the University of Iowa at Iowa City often disappeared from our services because many times they were absorbed into their service system. Communication between the two entities was poor at best.

Once other areas in the state learned what we had accomplished it inspired them to pursue similar projects. One area was successful in writing an even larger grant for even broader services. It was rewarding to see a vision come to fruition.

Professionally I was fine. But the valleys and hammers of the past were still haunting me. We were also in financial difficulty. I had a high profile title but in reality earning slightly over minimal wage. I had a wife and two children to support, and a loan for graduate school that now had to be repaid. The supposed friend of my Dad's who graciously funded my undergraduate degree now decided he wanted to be repaid. At the time he offered to pay for my college education there was no mention of his generosity being a loan. I had no problem with repaying him. It was only right. But the money just was not there. Judy did baby sitting in our home and I had two part-time jobs; and we were still struggling to make ends meet. It seemed a losing battle. We were getting nowhere.

# Chapter 38
## My Anger, Despair, and Hopelessness Surfacing to Meet the "still small voice"

I didn't realize my emotions were beginning to show. But, I am sure professionals in their respective specialties can recognize and understand my plight. The valley of unresolved grief was becoming too deep and the hammer of anger was causing more emotional pain. One day I was sitting on our front step just contemplating life, and wondering what I could do differently. I was not providing for my family the way I should, nor was I living up to the standards I had been taught by my parents as a child. Our neighbor, Wesley, happened to walk by and noticed me sitting there, but apparently I did not notice him. The next day we were visiting and Wesley mentioned that I truly looked dejected and depressed. He said, "You really looked low, indeed something must have been bothering you!" If he only knew! I probably changed the subject and continued with our visit. Unknowingly, I was in complete denial. That was the way I handled things back then. I suppressed it, stuffed it, and if need be I drove it down deeper into whatever valley of my despair happened to be ruminating in my psyche at the time. If it was obvious to Wesley, others must be noticing it also. Was I losing my ability to cope? Was I destined to follow in my mother's footsteps? Was I losing my mind? Was I no longer able to hide my true feelings? I was unaware that I was displaying the characterization of someone suffering from depression; despair, dejection, unhealed wounds, anger, unresolved grief, blaming God, lack of hope, fear that the next shoe will drop, worry, and absence of cheerfulness. Boy! If that isn't a medical diagnosis I don't know what is!

I remember I would get up very early in the morning usually around the crack of dawn. I was always an early riser. I would feel very angry. I felt indignation. I would have feelings of hostility reminiscent of years past during my youth. It didn't matter if it was someone or something I would often have feelings of ill will, hostility, hatred, and anger but had no way to vent these feelings. Just as I did when I was a child I would mentally try to plot how I could avenge or get even; but there was nothing or nobody with whom I could get even. Fortunately, I never carried out any of the sinister thoughts or plans I had conjured up in my mind against anyone knowingly, unless without my knowing it possibly could have surfaced at work or with family; and all the while I kept a mental black book in case I ever had the opportunity to use the plans I made to get even.

I was displaying signs of being emotionally disturbed and agitated. The valleys were stacking up one upon another; and the hammer blows had become more frequent with greater force leaving their tell tale marks, bruises, scars, and emotional pain. I was continuing to suppress all the lumps, bumps, and abrasions from rocks and other debris trying to work their way to the surface.

When I was younger one of the jobs I had was working for a concrete construction company. We did all kinds of concrete work. We did curb and gutter, sidewalks, driveways, basement floors, and a whole array of concrete projects. The addition to the junior college in Estherville, Iowa was one of our jobs. The fish hatchery at Spirit Lake, Iowa was another one of our jobs; and all of the curb and gutter for a new housing addition in Rock Rapids, Iowa was yet another of our projects.

Prior to pouring the actual concrete a lot of preparatory work needs to be done. A good firm base is needed. It has to be level. Then a porous layer like sand or gravel needs to be applied to aid in draining any moisture that may be under the concrete; and that also must be smooth and level. All of this work is done within the confines of sturdy forms so that once the concrete is poured it doesn't end up in your neighbor's yard, or the next zip code. Sometimes, after the concrete has been poured during the finishing process something gets in the way and comes to the top. It could be a rock, steel mesh, or anything that has worked its way to the surface of the concrete. The finishing cannot continue until that object is dealt with by removing it or forcing it below the surface of the concrete. That is exactly what I was doing with my feelings. I was suppressing or forcing from the surface all those emotional issues that become valleys from which I was so desperately trying to escape. Sometimes life can be like concrete. The stressors of everyday life can be the hammer. If one has ever dropped or purposely thrown a hammer against cured concrete it can be dangerous. Those things one has stuffed, tamped, poured, cured or hardened can be like finished concrete causing that hammer to bounce back and hit you.

God and I argued a lot back then. At least I called it arguing. It was always during prayer. I was trying to bargain with Almighty God! Late one night I remember praying to God, which at this point was a rare occurrence; and I said, "You've got to do something! If you don't step in and do something soon I don't know what is going to happen." His reply was, "David, you are not being honest, you are not being honest with Me, yourself, and everyone else." Not only was I shocked by His response but I was shocked by my anger, guilt, fear, and shame that I felt. God responded with that "still small voice" like he did with Elijah. I was no longer listening for that "still small voice." The full impact of that little encounter with The Almighty would not become evident until a few years later, and a number of times thereafter. From then on I began to listen much more closely to hear God's Voice.

Over time for me, God's voice is not an audible voice that anyone can hear. It is the presence of a perceived voice or message that is very clear and concise, and always relevant to my prayer. There is no mistaking it for anything other than a reply or a message. Elijah was in great distress and was told to listen for the Lord (1 Kings 19:11). There was a great and strong wind but the Lord was not in the wind. After the wind an earthquake, but the Lord was not in the earthquake; and after the earthquake a fire, but the Lord was not in the fire; and after the fire a 'still small voice'." Elijah heard it. I now listen for the "still small voice."

# Chapter 39
## VA Politics Don't Harmonize With My
## Personal Integrity Causing Emotional Turmoil

We left Burlington after three years. I accepted a position with the Veterans Administration at a V.A. Hospital in South Dakota as clinical audiologist and acting chief of the Audiology Speech Pathology Service. It was a good job with a lot more pay which was very much appreciated. But the job was demanding because it required having to fill two responsibilities. The role of Audiologist was easy because that's what I was trained to be. But the role of being in an administrative position was new territory for me. From day one it was on the job training. I didn't mind so much squeezing the paper work into my busy schedule, doing supervision, and other things that would come up with my clinical duties, but I quickly acquired a significant dislike for the politics.

Politics is a dirty business and is not limited to the government; I definitely learned that the hard way. We had an incident at our hospital when a patient was granted a weekend pass to be off station. He should not have been able to leave his hospital room let alone go off base and wander around town. While off station he got drunk and attempted to commit suicide by shooting himself. Fortunately, he was a very poor shot and survived. When an incident like that occurs with a patient or domiciliary resident the investigation is lead by V.A. staff, and not by local law enforcement. The local law enforcement cooperates but the V.A. takes the lead. The Center Director selects who he wants to investigate the incident. In this instance, he chose two individuals, one was my friend and the other was myself; probably because I was the new kid on the block. We got together and planned how we were going to proceed, and decided we would each conduct our own investigation, and when finished we would compare notes, and submit a report. Each of us then proceeded to do our investigations and everything went very well. We got together, compared notes and both of us came up with the same conclusion. If the patient would have been more closely supervised the whole incident could have been avoided, and that is what we submitted in our report. That did not look good for the V.A. When the Center Director read our report he became furious and told us we had no right to say that in our report, and there was no way he was going to wave "dirty laundry" in front of his superiors, the public, or anyone else, and we had better come up with a different report! My co-worker who I considered a friend, immediately said "You are right sir. We need to clean up the report." That left me hanging out on a limb. My principles and upbringing would not allow me to lie in a report or in any way shape or form state anything other than what the facts had determined. The report was rewritten but because of my belief that it was not true, and my "black and white" thinking at that time, I had to stand my ground and tell my boss, the Center Director, that for me to sign a report I knew was not true would be wrong and I could not sign it. Again he was furious and called me everything but my real name and said, "Next time we will get someone who has some intelligence!" From then on it was like I had the plague. I couldn't continue to consider my co-worker as a friend. I now felt like I was a leper!

Fortunately, after a couple years they were able to hire someone to fill the administrative portion of my position. That was fine with me, now I could devote all my time to the Audiology role that I was trained to do. But that whole experience began to gnaw at me. Here was a situation where a person could have lost his life because of a stupid mistake; and I was expected to sweep it under the rug as though it never happened. I would never have been able to justify such a thing. It was as if we were to say something like "Oh well, it's a good thing he didn't get hurt any worse than he did." What if he was to get another pass and was successful in killing himself or someone else? How does one rewrite and justify that report?

Judy and I talked about it and thought maybe it was time to leave. My position was a GS level position. For me to move to the next GS level would require a PhD which I did not have. There were pros and cons to leaving. I liked the area and the lifestyle. I had always liked the West. Hunting and fishing were good. I enjoyed the history and culture of the area. However, we were a long ways away from our families; one of which was my sister Rosemary, and Judy's family.

# Chapter 40

## Rosemary's Marriage is Abusive and Past Guilt Feelings From Being the Abusive 11 year old 'Man of the House' Surface

Rosemary marries and feelings of regret over my previous actions towards her surface. Judy, Ray and Opal, and I all saw red flags with marrying this particular guy; but the marriage took place, and she began to experience the consequences of this bad decision. She would frequently call me at all hours from Iowa to tell me what he had done, and ask me what I thought she should do. He was physically and verbally abusive. He saw pleasure in playing mean tricks on her. This guy was sick in the head!

My guilt over the way I had treated her when we were younger began to surface again. Was she thinking that what she was experiencing was normal because of the way I had treated her when we were younger? Was the way she was treated be considered as her normal? If that is the case; it is no wonder that one of the deep dark valleys I am in now is extreme guilt, and I can't find my way out. It is only right that I should be feeling such punishment for what I have done. The burden of such guilt is so heavy and almost unbearable.

One incident she related to me during one of her calls was especially disturbing. Rosemary's new husband had called her one night and said he was having trouble with his truck and would she come and pick him up. The location she was to meet him was hours away and she really didn't have enough money for gas, but she went anyway. She finally arrived there and began looking for him but couldn't find him. The location was a truck stop.

She looked for him inside and out and even drove around the area thinking he might be somewhere else close by. She searched for hours and never did find him or his truck. She asked inside if anyone had seen him. No one had seen him. She didn't know what to do so she drove back home hoping something bad hadn't happened, or perhaps he had somehow made it back home safely. After she arrived home he called her and said how funny it was to see her look for him. He had been there all the time watching her and there was nothing wrong with his truck. He thought it was a very funny joke! That, in addition to being physically abusive, was only one of the many mean things he did to Rosemary. That really made me angry but also raised my guilt another notch higher. Had I been 600 to 800 miles closer I probably would have let my former anger take over and done something really stupid, and I would be the one receiving justice instead of the one responsible for the mess she was now in. After that he looked at the telephone bill and saw all the long distance telephone calls and concluded she had been telling me what he was doing. She was then forbidden to call me. The only way she could call me was if she had an opportunity to use a pay phone or call me collect so most future calls were collect.

I think that incident along with my experience with the VA, and being closer to Judy's family was why we decided to leave. Perhaps by leaving it would open up an opportunity to pursue a doctoral degree which was something I now wished to pursue, but didn't ever seem to have the opportunity or finances. I resigned from the V.A., and we put our house that we liked so much up for sale, and prepared to move back to Iowa. I looked into doctoral programs and was accepted at the University of Nebraska at Lincoln. I was given an assistantship with a stipend and all of my previous coursework was accepted. I hadn't even started yet and my doctoral thesis topic was already approved. It looked like a slam dunk! Not so! Remember the valleys and hammers? It seems God had not yet chiseled away enough of what needed to be removed from me as a reminder of my honesty and my commitment to Him.

# Chapter 41
## I Am Slipping into the Valley of Despair, Searching for Work, Dire Finances, Bankruptcy, We Are On Welfare. New Baby Boy Joshua.

While in South Dakota Judy became pregnant and was having problems with her pregnancy. Is this going to be the same song only the next verse? We were temporarily back in Iowa and her delivery date was fast approaching. Now what do I do? No job, I hadn't started my assistantship yet so we had no income. With our savings gone, I had to swallow my Danish pride and ask for help. Never in my wildest imagination would I ever have thought I would need to go on welfare and food stamps. I hope I never have to go through such a demoralizing experience again. While on welfare, I did things and went places where I hoped nobody would recognize me. I went to grocery stores late at night hoping nobody would see me using food stamps. I parked my car where I hoped nobody I knew would see me.

Judy's medical problems continued and we had to make an emergency trip to Iowa City. About a week later Joshua was born on April 28, 1978. God was not finished chiseling away at me yet. Joshua had some health issues. In addition to being severely jaundiced he had high blood pressure and an irregular heartbeat. I had to make a decision whether I should go to Lincoln and hope the health issues resolve, or forego the PhD and find a job. I called my advisor in Lincoln and explained the situation. He told me I could postpone the PhD almost indefinitely but I would lose the assistantship and stipend. I decided the best thing to do was to look for a job. I felt that I had to generate some income so we could get off welfare. The problem was there was no job to be found. I used the profit from the sale of the house in South Dakota as a down payment on another house. Since I couldn't find a job, as a last resort, I took out a second mortgage on the house, and invested in a business. I thought I had checked the books of the business very well but I had missed one very important aspect. The business generated good revenue but the part I missed was that the income was quite seasonal. I didn't have enough funds to weather the lean time and the business was a failure. We had to cash in all of our life insurance, we lost what little savings was left, some of our possessions were auctioned off, the house was foreclosed on, and we had to declare bankruptcy. Bankruptcy in and of itself was a tremendous blow, and sank me even further into the valleys that were becoming deeper, steeper, darker; and I was still without a job. We had literally lost everything. I felt like I was in a deep dark pit and a complete failure. I felt so sorry for my wife and children for what they had to endure. Psalm 77 says "thou dost hold my eyelids from closing; I am so troubled that I cannot speak." Countless times, I for one, have felt as though the weight of every problem in the world was thrust upon me alone.

## My Suicide Is Planned

As a father and provider I felt like I was a complete failure. I was at the end of my rope. The valleys were too steep and too deep, my hope was gone, and my coping skills were depleting. I felt as if I had no place to turn but to give up. What my mother had done by committing suicide didn't seem so bad. I began to plan my way of demise. It had to be a way that would look like an accident, and it would have to take place at the right time, and right place for it to look like an accident. This would take some thought and some planning for it to be successful. For the next nine months I worked on my plan. By then the weather would be cold. Since I was using a neighbor's garage for our car, I would change oil in the car with the garage door open only enough to make it look like I was concerned about carbon monoxide but closed enough for poor ventilation. I would run the car to warm up the engine, and to circulate the oil in the engine. Then I would change the oil, start the car again to check for leaks, and just lay there until I slipped into eternity like my mother had done. It was April, 1979 when I had all my details worked out. Now all I had to do was wait for cold weather. The right weather condition never arrived.

## Chapter 42
## 3 Job Interviews Resulting in AEA 13 Late Hire as Audiologist, Intense Coworker Tension. I Am Losing my Grip and Sliding Into The Valley Below

It was late July or early August; I thought I would make one last attempt at finding a job. I think I called every area education agency in Iowa plus another university and some clinics. When I called Area Education Agency 13 to see if they had any openings I was told there was no vacancy at the present time, but they would send me an application in case a vacancy occurred. In the meantime, I learned of an opening in Des Moines and a teaching position at the University of South Dakota in Vermillion. I applied for all three hoping I would get the one at the University of South Dakota. It wasn't far from Vermillion to Lincoln and I could again pursue my PhD. I waited but no reply from any of them. Then one day all three called and wanted to know when I could come for an interview. I drove to Des Moines and Council Bluffs in one day, stayed with friends that evening, and drove to Vermillion the next day. Three interviews in two days might be a record. I even got lost and was late for the interview at AEA 13. At that interview I was asked how serious I was about the job and if I were offered the job that day would I take it? I said, "I have no job, a wife and three children to support. I am having three interviews in two days and I plan to take one of the three if it is offered!" I did not want the one in Des Moines, and they gave me the impression they did not want me anyway. That left AEA 13 and

South Dakota. A day or two later I received a call from the University of South Dakota informing me that they had decided on another applicant. I was very disappointed and dejected but called AEA 13 and told them I would take the job. I started August 1979.

We had no relatives in the area and didn't know anyone in Southwest Iowa. After looking at a map, I discovered there was a state park a few miles southeast of Harlan, Iowa. For about a month my address was Prairie Rose State Park where I pitched my tent. Things didn't seem so desperate anymore. During the week the park was a very peaceful place. I had the whole lake and park to myself. I got to know a fellow employee, also named David. He recently became divorced and was living in a mobile home in Harlan. David invited me to move in with him to share his mobile home for a few months while I continued looking for a house to rent since we were in no position financially to even consider purchasing a home. Rental homes, at the time, were scarce if available at all. We would need a house with at least two bedrooms, preferably three. About February I noticed an ad for a house for rent that appeared to be exactly what we needed. I called the telephone number and the owner, Mel, agreed to meet me there to show me the house. The house was very nice, clean, spacious, included a refrigerator and built-in stove with oven. That was great because we had lost all of our appliances earlier. It had a family room with a wood burning fireplace on the main floor and a finished basement with a pool table. There were three bedrooms on the main floor with a fourth in the finished basement. The house was in a nice neighborhood across the street from a city park and very close to church and schools. I asked what the rent would be and, unfortunately, it was more than we could afford. I tried to negotiate a lesser amount, but the amount he was asking was what he needed to make the mortgage payments on the house.

Mel and his wife had lived in another town, but originally were from the Harlan area. He had just retired and they were planning to return to Harlan. There was another house that they really liked but it wasn't for sale yet so they purchased this one. Shortly after purchasing the house I was looking at, the house they first liked came on the market again so they bought it

123

thinking this one would be easy to sell. It was empty for over a year and in the meantime his wife passed away. Now he was stuck with two houses and decided to try renting the one he showed me.

The house needed to be repainted and reshingled. Finally we were able to work out a deal. With sweat equity, if we would repaint the house and re-shingle the roof he would reduce the rent to an amount we could afford for six months. Without Judy or the kids even seeing it, I agreed to the terms on the spot in hopes that it would be acceptable.

March 1, 1980 we moved to 1416 Willow in Harlan. Mel kept his end of the bargain and so did we. We undertook the scraping and painting as a family. The roofing was done by myself and an occasional friend. The place had one drawback. There was a no garage, only a carport, and the driveway to the carport was a steep hill. I wondered what it would be like during the winter. I soon found out!

The steep driveway proved to be an interesting challenge. More than once we had to retrieve a vehicle from the park across the street because brakes would occasionally fail, a car would slip out of gear and into neutral, or because of ice and snow.

As time went on, I realized that the valleys of my past had not disappeared and that God was not finished with me yet. After a couple years a change in staff took place. The lady working for me finished her teaching degree and moved to Arizona. A replacement was hired against my recommendation, in spite of the fact that she had no prior experience. The person I recommended I knew could do the job because of previous experience. The director, in all his wisdom, chose the one with no experience. Unbelievable!

At first, things went relatively well. But as time went on friction developed and it became extremely difficult for us to work together. It seemed as though she thought she had my job and I supposedly had hers. I was the Audiologist; she was a Technician. Because of the friction we had to have separate work areas, and when we would be going to the same school at the same time we had to drive separate vehicles. Even though the tension between us was so thick you could practically cut it with a knife, I had no complaint with the quality of her work. She learned the job very quickly and was extremely efficient at what she did, but we could not work together.

I was assigned to approximately 50 different school buildings spread over a three county area. We were not hired by the school districts we served but by an intermediate agency, Area Education Agency 13, established by the state legislature to provide equal special educational services to these schools. This meant that when I was in a specific school I had an additional boss and countless teachers with whom to work. At times the job was overwhelming and the paper work insanely horrendous. But because of my work ethic, self-established high standards, my passion for the service being provided, and my driven personality, I pressed on while seemingly enjoying every moment.

It was not without a price. My family was suffering, not only financially because we were still trying to recover from what we had previously experienced; but the work related stress was causing old memories, thoughts, buried feelings, and long suppressed emotions to resurface again. The feelings of guilt, neglect, grief, anger, anxiety, inability to concentrate, difficulty sleeping and morbid thoughts all seemed to be attaining warp speed. I would lash out verbally for no apparent reason. The valleys had been rediscovered and I had not allowed God in to my circumstances. I no longer could hear that "still small voice" of God trying to speak to me. All I could hear were the rocks slipping and sliding beneath my hands and feet cascading down the valley wall to the bottom below, the dirt crumbling as I would lose my grip and footing; and the pain of falling in my desperate attempt to escape another valley of despair. Was I going insane? Would I ever escape or was I doomed to remain here for eternity. If this is what hell is like I want no part of it. "But He knows the way that I take; when He has first tried me, I shall come forth as gold" (Job 23:10). Lord, how much more are you going to try me? Will I soon be approaching the gold?

# Chapter 43
## Needed Vacation Turns Disastrous, Son's Life on Brink of Death

We finally had enough money to take a long overdue family vacation. Angela was 12, Sheila was 9 and Joshua was 3; so we thought Branson, Missouri and Silver Dollar City would be fun places to go. We left very early while it was still dark the morning of June 5, 1981 so the kids could sleep part of the way. Sometime later that morning we saw a McDonald's sign and decided it was time for breakfast. Later that day we finally reached our destination. Silver Dollar City was quite an experience. The rides were fun, some of the demonstrations were very interesting, as were some of the shops. I especially enjoyed the woodcarving shop and the gun shop. It was a fun-filled day for all. We decided to check into our motel since it had been a rather long day. We drove back to Branson, got something to eat, and checked into our motel to get a good night's rest. We had planned a full schedule for the next couple days.

The motel had an outdoor swimming pool so the girls, Josh, and I decided to take advantage of the pool before going to bed. Josh and I were the first to get out of the pool and return to our motel room. I got dressed and Judy got Josh ready for bed in his brand new Sesame Street pajamas. Our motel room was on the third floor with a balcony the full length of the motel in front of each room. Josh and I decided to go out on the balcony to watch the girls swim. Being on the third floor I was rather nervous for the safety of the children even though the balcony did have a steel railing. I had instructed the children that there would be no running, no climbing on the railing, and no clowning around. They all understood and obeyed. Josh and I were standing on the balcony leaning against the motel exterior wall away from the railing with Josh next to me on my left. As I was looking at Josh one of the girls yelled "Hey Dad, watch this one." I looked toward the pool just in time to see Angela jump off the diving board; and I immediately looked back to my left to make sure Josh was still where he was a nanosecond ago. Much to my horror all I saw was him going through the space of the railing as though being shot from a cannon and falling to the concrete parking lot below. To this day, I do not know how Josh was thrust feet first toward and through the railing. My first instinct was to leap over the railing after him; but soon realized that was not a good idea. I raced to the stairs as fast as I could. I don't recall if I used any of the steps; if I did there were very few. All the way down the three flights of stairs I knew he was going to be dead. How was I going to tell Judy and the girls that our little boy, their little brother Josh, was dead? I was already thinking about how we were going to plan his funeral.

I found him lying face down unconscious on the concrete next to someone's van. I instinctively checked for a pulse and was both relieved and surprised he had a heartbeat. How could anyone survive such a fall? I yelled for someone to call an ambulance and immediately one of the other guests rushed out to offer assistance. They heard me yelling and had already called for an ambulance. Judy and the girls arrived and Judy was beside herself, next to hysterical. The wife of the man who rushed to my aid took Judy aside and began praying with her, and everyone was crying and comforting each other. I again checked for a pulse and it was still there. I felt his head and immediately felt a mushy area of his head. I knew he had a massive skull fracture and we had a very desperate situation on our hands. Was our three year old son going to die right there on the concrete? After what seemed an eternity the ambulance finally arrived. The emergency crew quickly took charge, attached telemetry to Josh and loaded him into the ambulance. One of the crew gave me directions to the hospital and they left. The girls quickly got dressed and we were on our way to the hospital.

When we arrived at the hospital Josh was already in the emergency room being seen by a doctor. We waited in the empty waiting room. It was about 10:00PM and Josh had been in the emergency room for quite some time and nobody came out to give us any report of Josh's condition. Then a nurse came from another direction. She walked up to us, introduced herself telling us her name, and said she understood that our 3 year old son had been injured and asked if she could pray with us. We said "yes" and afterward she said that her son who had a similar injury to Josh survived fine, and she felt that like her son, our son Josh would also be OK. Then the doctor came out to talk with us and she was gone. I tried to see which direction she had gone but it appeared she had just vanished. The doctor said that Josh had a massive skull fracture, was stable for now, but must be transferred to the trauma center for neurosurgery. Josh was placed back into the ambulance and made ready for the 50 mile trip to Springfield. Before leaving, one of the emergency crew members gave us directions to Cox Trauma Center in Springfield, Missouri. He also told us not to try to keep up with them, and if we saw them stopped along the road not to be alarmed because they would probably be making routine stops to check Josh's vital signs.

I started thinking about the nurse we saw and how she had prayed with us. There was something peculiar about her. First of all it was her uniform. This was 1981 and she was wearing a nurse's uniform that certainly was not from the 1981 period. It was more like one that would have been worn 40, 60, or maybe 80 years ago. It was very long and almost touched the floor. Her nurse's hat was also from a different era; it was tall with high pointed peaks. The second thing I noticed about her uniform was that it was so wrinkled it looked like it had been packed in a laundry basket untouched for decades, or maybe even for a century! The third thing was that we never saw her walk away. She just seemed to disappear. I didn't think any more about it. I was more interested in getting us to Springfield.

We left for Springfield following the directions that I had been given. We did see the ambulance stopped along the road once; but soon it passed us and we never saw it again. At one point we had to drive through a driving rainstorm. It rained so hard we could hardly see where we were going. We were given excellent directions and finally arrived at Cox Trauma Center in Springfield. After parking the car we entered the emergency area waiting room. It was totally empty and had kind of an eerie feeling about it. Josh was already being seen when we arrived. I tried to read but couldn't concentrate. The only thing on television was one of those endless loop things showing the temperature, barometric pressure, wind direction, amount of precipitation, and would occasionally be interrupted by a commercial. I walked over to the emergency room doors hoping to hear something about Josh's condition. All I heard was someone talking to someone else about a stabbing that had occurred earlier that evening. The wait seemed endless and it was approaching 2:00AM or was it 3:00AM. Anyway the time of day didn't seem to matter. What did matter was for somebody to tell us something about our Josh.

Finally a doctor came out to talk to us. He introduced himself and told us that although Josh was stable for the moment, he was very sick and could die. He told us that Josh had suffered a massive skull fracture with probable associated brain damage; and that the next 48 hours would be critical. If Josh could make it through the next 48 hours he would have a better chance of survival. The doctor was not overly optimistic nor was he overly pessimistic. He was just honest with the facts. We appreciated that. I needed to contact relatives about what had happened to Josh. I called my sister and she started to call other relatives who in turn called someone else. I couldn't call our pastor because we didn't have one. When we moved to Harlan the church we had planned to join was going through a call process so there was no pastor to call. We were really in need of the power of prayer but who could I call. I had recently joined The Optimist Club in Harlan. I remembered one of the members was a pastor. I called Pastor Yancy and told him who I was and why I was calling. He was very reassuring and told me not to worry. He in turn called another Optimist Club member who happened to be a pastor also, but was presently not serving any church. Between the two pastors what they accomplished was truly remarkable.

Within days they had organized a prayer chain from coast to coast and were able to somehow financially support us the whole time we were there. Judy called a friend she had recently met in Harlan. It turned out she had a pastor brother who was serving a church right here in Springfield. As a result, Pastor Henry came and was a great comfort to us all.

Josh was moved to the Children's ICU and we were told that we could be there with Josh as much as we wanted, but they would prefer that we not stay more than five minutes each time. Later they waived the five minute rule and let us stay as long as we wanted because the staff didn't think he would survive the night. It was rather shocking to see him the first time in the intensive care Unit. He was in a coma and hooked up to all kinds of tubes and telemetry, his face was all swollen, he was beginning to bruise, and the fracture on the side of his head was very evident. We took turns for the five minute stay while the rest of us searched for the waiting room hoping to find a place to rest. When we found the waiting room it was packed and sometimes there was standing room only. The only chairs to sit on were chrome steel chairs with very little cushion. Periodically people would leave their seats, and someone would immediately take their place. Eventually we were able to get two chairs so we took turns holding the girls on our laps until another chair became vacant. We asked a nurse if we could have one or two pillows for the girls and we were told they were all taken.

The next day I took Angela with me and returned to the motel in Branson. We had left in such a hurry the night before we had left everything in our room. We packed up everything, loaded it in to the car and stopped at the motel office to check out. We stopped to get something to eat, and since the hospital was on the way out of town we also made a stop there. I wanted to see if I could get the top to Josh's new pajamas that had been removed the night before, and if possible, I wanted to thank the nurse who had prayed with us. I located two staff members, told them who we were, and that Josh had been treated there the previous evening. I asked if it was possible to have Josh's new pajama top. The nurse checked to see if she could find it but they had already disposed of it. Then I asked about the nurse. They asked me what her name was. I told them her name, that she had prayed with us, and I wanted to thank her. There was a long pause, they looked mysteriously at each other, and finally one of them said "Sir, there hasn't been anyone by that name who has worked here in years!" Dumbfounded we left for Springfield. I still felt there was something strange about that nurse. After returning to Springfield, and relating our experience to Judy at the Branson hospital, we could only come up with one explanation; it had to be some type of divine intervention, or possibly an angel!

The waiting room at first was a lonely place. You could tell by the look on the faces of the people who were there that they were deeply concerned about someone. Gradually we would get to know some of the people there. We would exchange stories of what brought us there. We met and prayed with a woman whose father was dying and with the family of a young man who had been accidentally run over by a boat while water skiing. The prop of the boat motor had struck him on the head. We learned about a young boy who had fallen from the back of a pickup. Everyone had a story to tell. Even though each one was different, they were all very serious and important as if they were part of our family. Pretty soon all of us were becoming more like a community. We would pray with one another or pray for someone specifically. There was a telephone in the room and if it rang anyone would answer. If the caller wanted to talk to any of us there the person who answered the phone would announce who the call was for. A kind of bonding took place there. We became a rather close knit little community. I would later refer to it as a Christian Community in Action.

For two weeks our address was Cox Trauma Center and we were sitting on our chrome steel chairs in Springfield, Missouri where we lived while Josh was hospitalized. Josh remained in a coma for almost five days. He started to arouse and become agitated sometime during the fifth day. The next day he was moved to a room with another young boy who was recovering from some kind of abdominal surgery.

Once he was fully awake I become very concerned. The Josh I saw was not the Josh we knew. He had difficulty speaking and his speech was slurred. When he tried to say "Mom" it was "Om". He had always loved to watch Sesame Street and knew the names of all the characters. Now he couldn't identify or recognize the names of any of the characters. He had difficulty walking. Would we ever have back the Josh that we once knew? It was heart-wrenching!

We met some very nice and interesting people during our two week stay there. The father of the young boy in Josh's room was missing a hand and wrist that he lost when his hand got caught in a sorghum machine. Down the hall from Josh was another young boy with a severely fractured leg from being trapped in a log pile while playing. We met both of his parents and some of his relatives. They were all Amish and very nice friendly folks. While talking with the father I learned, in addition to his row crops, he raised turkeys. He even showed me pictures of his huge, new turkey building. It was quite impressive. Of course nobody was pictured in the photograph, just the building and the turkeys. Cindy, a young girl of about 10 to 12 years of age would be sitting in a wheelchair every day in the hallway near the nurse's station. Cindy was the sole survivor of her family that had an auto accident. She had sustained massive head trauma in addition to other injuries. It was so sad to see her sitting there day after day and not able to communicate. The only visitor I ever saw with her on a regular basis was I think a pastor. He would come very often, talk to her, read some scripture and pray. Not knowing her receptive skills I don't know how much she understood, comprehended, or even heard what he had been saying. I often wonder what happened to Cindy. There was a young boy about 8 to 10 years of age. He and his family had been to a home supply center to purchase some sheets of plywood. The plywood was too wide to lay flat in the back of their pickup so they placed it as flat as possible lying against one side of the pickup box. The young boy was riding in the back of the pickup sitting on the plywood. Apparently on their way home a gust of wind somehow caught the edge of the plywood and the young boy was scooped out of the pickup landing on the road. He sustained head trauma and was still in a coma when we left two weeks later. I often wonder about him also and I grieve for those children and their parents. We were extremely blessed to be able to take our Josh home with us even though valleys, challenges, and probably some chiseling still lay ahead of us.

# Chapter 44
## My son Josh Struggles with Brain Injury and Overcomes with God's Grace and Healing and Lots of Hard Work and Perseverance on his Part

After returning home Josh's walking improved and eventually he was running and playing like any three year old. His pronunciation gradually improved and soon he was talking and articulating as though he had never been injured. He did frequently have a problem with word retrieval which would frustrate him a great deal. We had to watch him for seizures. At age three and on to age five he couldn't understand why he was unable to express what he was thinking. Afterwards he would become frustrated with what he wanted to say but couldn't, and then his response would be "Just forget it." Otherwise we thought he was doing extremely well. He seemed no different than any other active three year old boy. He went to a private preschool and attended a regular public kindergarten.

It wasn't until the second semester of first grade that his brain injury became evident. The teacher labeled him as a discipline problem because he just would not do his work. When he turned in his paper work it was always unfinished. He was not disruptive in the classroom; in fact he would sit like a perfect little gentleman. We knew he was not defiant and did not display behaviors that would suggest discipline problems. We had no answer nor did any of the special education staff as to why he was not doing his work. He seemed to understand the work but just was not doing it. One has to remember this was early and somewhat unknown territory in the field of special education with regard to traumatic head injuries.

One day the light bulb came on purely by accident! Josh had a good friend named David and they would play a lot together. One day they were playing the game "Battleship" which is a game where each player tries to guess or figure out where their opponent's ships are located and sink them. It requires placing pegs either in a horizontal plane or vertical plane. After playing the game for awhile, David came to Judy and said "Josh is cheating. He doesn't put the pegs where he is supposed to." It wasn't that Josh was cheating or did not know how to play the game; he had played the game numerous times before. Judy went to check to see what the problem might be. She checked both David's and Josh's playing boards and at first everything seemed in order. They each had their ships placed in their respective hiding places on the horizontal or flat portion of their game boards. But when she compared the placement of the pegs where hits should have been indicated something was not quite right. Josh didn't have any pegs placed in the vertical portion of his playing board; all of his were down in the horizontal area. What was going on here? After some extensive investigations and evaluations, it was discovered that Josh could not transfer from a vertical plane to a horizontal plane and vise versa. He also had difficulty being able to cross a midline both vertically and horizontally, and his visual depth perception was seriously impaired. That explained why he never finished his work! The teacher would place on the blackboard what the students were to copy at their desks. Josh was unable to do the task of transferring what was on the blackboard to his paper at his desk. Various techniques were used to help Josh, like paper with raised physical lines so he could know where he was on his paper. His difficulty with word retrieval was becoming more evident. When his teacher would ask him a question it would many times take him so long to process the question, formulate a response in his mind and make a reply, that she would accuse him of not paying attention. All of this combined is how she arrived at the conclusion that he was a discipline problem. At the beginning of each school year we would ask the teacher to be watchful for seizures and any signs of his brain injury and possible related side effects.

As time went on school became more challenging and more difficult. It was not uncommon for us to be up until 10:00PM or later trying to help him complete his homework. There were many tearful nights with Josh saying "I can't do this" or "Don't make me do this anymore." It was heart wrenching to see him try so hard; but he didn't give up. It was not only hard for Judy and me, but for his older sisters as well who looked after him and were his protectors.

There were also some holes in his knowledge base resulting from the injury. One instance when Josh was in high school that was amusing, but also indicates how pervasive head injuries can be, was when we received a "Down-Letter" from the school indicating that Josh was failing P.E. I contacted the school to find out why he was not passing P.E. I was told he had not been showing up for P.E. so they had no choice but to notify us with the "Down-Letter." I asked Josh how he could not be passing P.E. and his response was "I showed up for P.E. but nobody was there." After checking into the situation a little further we were able to solve the dilemma. On the window of the office there would be a sign for each day that would either say "Even" or "Odd" to let the students know which day they would have P.E. Josh didn't know the difference between "Even" or "Odd." His vision and visual perception were also affected by the injury. To this day he continues to have difficulty determining distances. He still has difficulty with word retrieval but has learned to compensate for it so well that it is not noticeable. The average person who did not know that Josh had sustained any type of head injury would not notice anything different about Josh.

Academics continued to be a struggle for him and he did receive special help through a special education resource teacher. On one occasion, through sheer determination, he did make the honor roll. We were so proud of him.

There were some valleys because of some very bad decisions he made while associating with the wrong group of individuals he thought were friends. Reminiscent of my own teen years, Josh had some experiences with local law enforcement. Working with Josh, I began to better understand my own teen years and slowly diffuse some of my own anger by being patient and loving with Josh, my own dear son. We became very familiar with laws related to drinking and drug use, especially as a minor; and as an adult in treatment programs. We know what it is like to have our son arrested. We know what it is like to have our son in jail. We know what it is like to have our son in treatment programs. During these years, I was able to do for Josh what I wish my dad could have done for me. By persevering with him through his difficulties with schoolwork, we were able to reinforce in him the importance of education and working up to one's capacities. I was able to hold onto the prayer connection between Heaven and earth and plead for my son. Loving him through his troubles with the law and addictions, caused us to pray deeply and in faith for his recovery in ways that have blessed our own spiritual lives. We overflow with gratitude to God that He answered our prayers beyond what we asked. God has taught me values and shaped my character by taking me through the consequences of wrong choices; my own and Josh's. Josh and I are walking together with Christ through a valley as pictured on the book cover.

Today Josh is doing very well. He has a good paying full-time job, has purchased a condo and lives with his cat in Iowa City, Iowa. He loves to hunt and fish and if you have any questions about sports he is a walking encyclopedia.

# Chapter 45
## Surprised By a New Family Home,
## A Fixer Upper With Potential

In 1992 we were approached by the wife of a friend of ours who was an agent with one of the local realtors. She found us a house that was in foreclosure and urged us to take a look at it. We were still renting from Mel, and because of what we had gone through financially, we didn't think that purchasing a home again was even a possibility. Camille convinced us to look at it with an open mind; and seemed positive that this house should be our next house! On the way to the house she cautioned us that since it had been empty and unlived in for a couple years, we should think of its possibilities and potential. To say I was shocked at seeing this gross place, would be an understatement! It was a filthy mess with loose wallpaper hanging down everywhere! We went upstairs to look at the two bedrooms up there. In one of them a large piece of wallpaper was hanging from the ceiling, and when I reached up to pull it free a huge section of ceiling plaster came down with it.

Things were not looking very favorable. We proceeded to the basement, but because there were no utilities we could not see it very well. I did notice that someone had put in a great deal of money and effort to install a hardwood floor and paneling in one room in the basement. Even though the place was a real mess, I could see it had potential, but I didn't say anything. She realized that the place looked pretty bad but she also said "You are a handy person and you could have this place looking very nice in no time at all." Basically she was correct. What the house needed was a thorough cleaning, old wallpaper removed, some painting, and the repairs were things I could do myself. Silently I was beginning to agree with her, but so far Judy had not said much. When we asked what the price was we were surprised at the extremely low price considering the neighborhood in which it was located. She said it was because the house was in foreclosure and had not sold in three or four years.

We left there with mixed emotions about the house and the finances. We thought about it, talked about it, prayed about it; and finally decided to talk to one of Judy's friends who happened to be a loan officer at one of the local banks. She told us that the mortgage would be no problem. The previous owner had financed the home with a VA loan and all we had to do was assume the balance of the loan. God was still working. The down payment and closing costs were the problem, but Judy's friend, the loan officer, arranged to loan us the balance of what was needed if we would pay down what we could.

We signed the necessary papers, gave Mel our thirty day notice, and began the arduous job of making an inhabitable house into a habitable home. It was an awful job. Judy would spend what free time she had doing what she could. The girls would do what they could do after school if they didn't have homework. Josh was too little so he became our supervisor! After work I would be there until wee hours in the morning. Even though we were not able to accomplish everything we wanted to do we moved in Thanksgiving weekend 1992. Twenty six plus years later we are still here.

# Chapter 46

## My Medical Concerns. Mental Health Incidents and Spiritual Depression. Life Changing Accident and Cascading Down to Another Valley

For me, it seemed, the harder I worked the more stressed I became. I could see that I was beginning to weaken emotionally. At times I would be rude, forgetful, had trouble sleeping, felt paranoid, and argumentative. I would frequently fall asleep while driving, and often felt incompetent in what I was doing. I would be short and snappy to people for no reason. I began to wonder if I really needed to exist.

One evening Judy and I attended a session on mental health. It was my ploy to get Judy to go because I was convinced that she might need counseling. At the end of the session everyone was given a mental health screening. Judy passed the screening with flying colors. I was told to make an appointment with my family doctor the next day. I made the appointment and in a couple days saw my doctor. I told him about our experience and that I was told to see him. He asked me, "Do you now, or have you ever felt like hurting yourself, or someone else?" When I answered "yes" he immediately wrote out a prescription for anti-depression medication. After numerous follow up visits the medication was gradually increased to the maximum dose. I was doing much better, but I wasn't out of the woods yet. My doctor felt I should be seeking additional professional help and experience some emotional healing that needed to take place. This guidance was probably from that "still small voice" that I had been neglecting to listen to lately.

There was a benefit available through my employer AEA 13 called the "Employee's Assistance Program." It was basically a five session counseling program made available free of charge to employees. The employee would meet with one of the counselors for mental health evaluation, and to discuss issues that may be affecting you personally and your performance at work. At the end of the five sessions the counselor would determine whether or not one needed further sessions, or referral to someone like a psychiatrist. I took advantage of the program numerous times and each time I was dismissed. I don't know if the counselors were under trained and therefore unable to see enough red flags to warrant further sessions and evaluations, or if they felt that I did not need any further intervention. If truth were told, I was not listening to God. Whatever the case, I was again feeling the chiseling and chipping away at my psyche. I did feel that I was near a slippery slope cascading down to another valley.

Incidents and accidents, which I will go into further detail later, occurred that forever changed my life and the lives of those around me. This continued for a number of years.

The first was an incident, although totally by accident, and not related whatsoever; but yet very reminiscent, and similar to the plan I had hatched some years prior as a way to end all and slip into eternity. Some may have thought otherwise but this was purely an accident. I had been working on my pickup. I had to replace the clutch plate, pressure plate, a bearing in the transmission, and the resurfaced flywheel put back into place. I was almost finished. All I had left to do was reinstall the driveshaft and adjust the clutch. As I was attaching the bolts holding the driveshaft's U-joint to the rear differential, the pickup came crashing down, crushing me and pinning me under the pickup. I was pinned so tightly I could not move to free myself. I was held down in such a way that my chest was compressed making it impossible to inhale or exhale, and I was slowly running out of air. I was also in excruciating pain from fractured ribs and numerous internal injuries. Fortunately it was a nice day. The garage door, as well as the house windows were open; and numerous neighbors were out mowing their lawns. It was also fortunate that a number of things occurred at the right place and the right time or I would not be here today. Judy was talking to a friend on the telephone who happened to be familiar with handling 911 calls. While talking she thought she heard a strange noise from the garage. Judy told the person she was going to check on the noise which came from the garage and she would be right back. When she saw that I was trapped beneath the pickup she returned to the telephone, and told the person to immediately call 911 and send an ambulance. Judy yelled at a neighbor who quickly rushed to my aid, but injured his back trying to lift the pickup to take some of the weight off from me, but was unable to do so. He yelled to the neighbors who were out mowing their lawns to come and help. In the meantime one of our local physicians happened to be jogging by, noticed the commotion, and crawled under the pickup to check my vital signs. The neighbors came running just as the emergency crew arrived; and there were enough men to lift the pickup just high enough while others pulled me out just as I became unconscious due to lack of air. I was immediately transported to our local hospital where I was examined by the doctor on call. The emergency crew had given me oxygen and by the time we arrived at the hospital I was almost fully awake. The attending physician, after quickly checking me over, told me to stand, and asked if it hurt to stand. I replied that I hurt all over. He asked again "Does it hurt when you stand?" I replied just the same. He said "I don't think you are hurt too badly you can go home."

Even though on occasion I would jokingly accuse Judy of being "mass hysteria looking for a place to land," that evening being no exception, she seldom becomes angry to the point where she expresses an opinion. She has always been stable as a rock and very level-headed. That evening was different. She yelled, "Like hell he's going home. You're going to keep him!" Way to go Jude!

I was admitted and kept overnight for observation and released the next day. Either during the accident, that evening, or the next day, I experienced a stroke. I had petechiae (pe-teek-ee-eye) so severely that my eyes were totally red, my body was filling up with fluid and was suffering with pain. I was beginning to look like the Pillsbury Doughboy with Satanic red eyes!

# Chapter 47
## Starting the Long Journey Back Physically and Emotionally. Medtronic Pain Stimulator.

A few miserable days later Judy and our oldest daughter Angela took me to Omaha. We just picked a doctor at random. My doctor was a young whipper-snapper who looked like he had just graduated from medical school. He ordered X-rays, did a thorough examination, and left the room to review the X-rays. When he returned he said, "You have fractured ribs and I am concerned about more injuries so I am going to admit you, just sit tight." I was immediately admitted to Clarkson Hospital. I had fractured ribs on my left side, and numerous internal injuries; a bruised heart, a bruised lung, a bruised liver, damaged kidneys, and a portion of my lymphatic system had been destroyed. And to think that the attending ER physician the evening of the accident was just going to send me home.

After a few days of treatment I was well enough to go home. After a couple weeks I could tell something still was not quite right and went to see my regular local doctor. By then I had begun to fill up with fluid again and was hospitalized a second time. I was subjected to a series of tests and in addition to the fluid they found a blood clot in one leg. After being treated there for about a week I was well enough to go home again.

For a couple months I felt pretty good except I couldn't get rid of pain in my legs and fluid had again returned to my legs. I was even able to reattach the driveshaft on my pickup and finish the job I had started months before. Because I was still having fluid and pain in my legs I again returned to my local doctor. He said, "This whole incident has been very hard on you." He referred me to Mayo Clinic for a second opinion. I was seen and treated by two good hospitals in Omaha, and supposedly by some of the country's best at Mayo Clinic in Rochester, Minnesota, and I was told nothing is wrong, go home and find a pain clinic. I was feeling pretty discouraged.

After arriving home I made an appointment with a pain clinic in Council Bluffs. The doctor reviewed my records and test results, and suggested an epidural shot. He gave me the epidural shot and for the first time I could stand up straight, totally pain free and could walk with no assistance. Praise the Lord, why couldn't this have been done months ago! Unfortunately, it only lasted one week. I went back to the same doctor and told him the results. He suggested a second shot. After the shot I felt the same as I did after getting the first shot, totally pain free. That one lasted one month. I went back a third time to the same doctor. This time he was not as encouraging as before. He told me he could not give me another shot this soon; one can only have so many within a certain time period. But, he told me he could refer me to someone else who has a slightly different procedure and perhaps he could be of help. We made the appointment and he gave me some kind of injection and bingo! I was pain free again; but only for three months.

By now the summer was gone, school was starting, and it was time for me to go back to work. I went back to my family doctor who gave me a prescription for pain when I needed it, and told me he was sorry he could not do more.

I decided to go back to the internist who treated me at Clarkson. He prescribed other medications for my pain one of which was a narcotic patch. The combination of medications did help control my pain, but at times the pain was still so severe I almost had to vomit. I returned to the internist and he increased the dosage of the medication. The down side was that I was not supposed to drive. Now I had to rely on someone to get me to and from my schools. I tried to arrange rides with other staff members who happened to be going to the same school or at least a school nearby. Judy also served as my taxi driver when she could. Eventually the increase in dosage was no longer effective.

In the meantime, at a family reunion, a relative who works for Medtronic told me about an electronic device they manufacture that helps control chronic pain. An appointment was made for me to see the neurosurgeon. After going through my history he told me that I might be a candidate for this electronic device and asked me if I would be interested in using one on a trial basis. If it turned out to be successful he could surgically implant the device. It turned out to be the very same device I learned about from my cousin. I agreed to try this gizmo and he scheduled me for surgery. Two electrodes were implanted in my spine and I had wires protruding from my back that went into a small box-shaped device that I wore around my waist. At the end of the trial period I returned to report if I thought it was effective. It was effective for certain parts of my legs but not effective for other areas. He told me that adjustments could be made to the instrument to change the area of coverage, and that I would also have a remote control which would allow me to make some adjustments myself. With the remote control I could turn it on or off and also adjust the intensity. By now I was willing to try almost anything so I agreed to have the whole thing implanted.

My surgery was scheduled a couple days before Thanksgiving. The surgery went well and on Thanksgiving Day a young lady came to my hospital room. She introduced herself, said she is from Lincoln, Nebraska and would program my new electronic pain control stimulator. I was quite impressed that someone would drive from Lincoln, Nebraska on Thanksgiving Day just to adjust my new electronic gizmo that was securely placed near my waist under my skin on my right side. She had me hold a small disk over the device which was connected to a hand held computer-like device. She proceeded to press buttons, make adjustments, and frequently would ask how it felt; does it help, and does it cover the right area. It was a rather lengthy trial and error process and then all of a sudden she hit pay dirt. I was feeling what seemed like a very mild electric shock over the pain area and I was no longer feeling as much leg pain as I had previously. It didn't completely remove the pain but it certainly made it tolerable. With the pain medication and the new device I was again able to function physically, but emotionally it was a different story.

# Chapter 48
## My Hope is Gone, Despair at Warp Speed, Heritage House Again, "I can do all things through Christ who strengthens me" Philippians 4:13

The Medtronic gizmo was working but emotionally I was losing my grip more and more. I went numerous times to the Employee Assistance Program but never saw the same person twice. I finally decided it was a waste of time. Every day while trying to climb out of my valleys I kept slipping backward with each new attempt. I finally realized in all fairness to my family, I needed professional help because they were also suffering and hurting because of me. But I didn't know where to go until I remembered that a family friend had told me about a woman therapist she used to see and really liked. She gave me her telephone number and I gave her a call. When the therapist answered, I told her who I was and asked if I could see her. Her first response was "How did you get my home telephone number?" I told her and she said "I figured it had to be her and yes I can see you." She gave me an appointment at her office with the Willow Group located in Council Bluffs.

I'm not sure our first visit was the best or worst possible time together. Actually it was both. She immediately started to ask me questions. Some were easy to answer and some were difficult and painful to answer. All during the interview she was taking notes like crazy. The more we talked I could tell for the first time, I was talking to someone who not only understood me, but really seemed to care and wanted to help. I saw her a couple more times but unfortunately my anti-depression medication was not working well and I knew I needed immediate help. I could not go on! I asked her about hospitalization and if she could recommend a good psychiatrist. I knew at that point I was about to break. Any hope I ever had was gone. Despair was at warp speed, and any strength to cope had long since evaporated. I had to cancel my next appointment with her because I became suicidal, and my family had to admit me to the emergency psych ward "Heritage House" at Immanuel Hospital in Omaha Nebraska.

That first night was horrible. I had become addicted to the narcotic pain medications from my near fatal injury, and I should have been seen quite some time ago for psychiatric care because of my troubled and painful past. They took away all my medications cold turkey, and that first night I thought I would have to get better to die. I was nauseated, I hurt, I couldn't sleep, and I paced the halls for hours. I thought morning had been cancelled for lack of interest! I didn't eat anything for about two days for fear it wouldn't stay down.

The staff there was excellent and they knew how to care for people like myself. The psychiatrist I initially saw is the Director of Heritage and I continue to see him periodically to this day. During my week at Heritage House he told me "We don't keep you here until you're cured, we keep you here until you are better so that when you go home you can begin to put into practice some of the things you will learn here." There were numerous classes to attend, and sessions where we would share various aspects of our lives; our feelings, and especially learn about ourselves. My medications were adjusted and/or changed, and I was prescribed a different antidepressant. I was released with instructions for a follow up appointment with the psychiatrist.

After being released from the psych ward, I tried to contact the therapist I had seen prior to going to Heritage. Much to my disappointment I learned that the Willow Group had disbanded and I was never able to find her again. I did learn that some of the people she had worked with chose to work with Horizon Therapy, so I made an appointment there in hopes of getting good ongoing therapy. Through Horizon I met and worked with an excellent therapist who also understood, cared deeply about me, and helped me work through issues of my past and my life. She is a Christian which I value very highly. Beatriz had a small plaque in her office proclaiming "I can do all things through Christ who strengthens me" (Philippians 4:13) which happened to be one of my favorite Bible verses. It has been an anchor for me for many years. It took many years for this scripture to become an inner realization that I could live by. She helped me a great deal during the years I worked with her. I continued to see her until June 2012 when she left to take a new position in another state.

The psychiatrist I saw at Heritage, continued to try various medications for my depression. One or two of the medications were a disaster resulting in return visits to Heritage a second and third time. During my second stay at Heritage a medication was finally found to be effective at maximum dose, and I continued to take it until recently when he decided to change my medication again. My new medication seemed to have a learning curve but I am now doing quite well.

A humorous event occurred during one of my stays at Heritage when my late boss and supervisor and his wife came to visit me one evening. He is a polio survivor confined to an electric wheelchair. He also has a tracheotomy and uses a respirator to breathe. Shortly before they were about to leave a young nurse came into my room. She walked over to my visitor, placed her hand on his shoulder and said, "Are you ready for your bath or shower?" I'm sure that young lady was mortified when I had to explain to her that I was the patient.

## Chapter 49
## Where Is God When I Need Him the Most?

Where is God when I am depressed and really in need? Short answer! He is going through my struggles with me and extending His tenderest mercy with the least amount of pain possible so that I can be free. Why do I continue to struggle believing that? Remember those words God spoke to me years ago? "David, you are not being honest!" What now? God has been merciful to me so that by faith I can see His Love and Mercy over my life. Am I cured? I am stable; I have some big scars that once were wounds but do not hurt as before. Am I better? Yes, I am not struggling. Do I blame God for what He allowed in my life? I see that God has used circumstances that He has allowed in my life for healing which is a lot different than being angry at God over what He has done to me. Do I still have peaks and valleys? Yes, everyone has normal ups and downs and mine are in that range. At times when I ask the question "Why do I still hurt? the answer is contradictory because I hurt less and more. The hurt in my body is under control, but hurt can also have the purpose of more healing through pruning which may hurt. Jesus describes it this way. "I am the true vine and my Father is the vinedresser. Every branch of mine that bears no fruit, he takes away, and every branch that does bear fruit he prunes that it may bear more fruit" (John 15:1-2). Sometimes I hurt because God is pruning me so that I may be more like Him while He is using my circumstances to bring about spiritual growth. It hurts to be pruned! As written, the branch needs to be pruned in order to bear more fruit.

It is usually easy and uncomplicated to see the unpleasant sensations associated with physical pain. Conversely, psychological pain sometimes takes years for symptoms to appear, and many times there are no immediate visible effects from the time of the initial assault and even with treatment. Covering many aspects of emotional distress, psychological pain identifies the three underlying causes as; unexpressed anger and fear, guilt and shame, depression and anxiety. Mental suffering and emotional pain are real, debilitating, and unrelenting.

For me it was almost too late. During those times of deep valleys with seemingly no means of escape, I saw myself think and do some pretty strange things. Some of which are still too tender or painful to discuss. My age indicated that I was finally an adult, yet emotionally I was still an eleven year old youngster stuck in an adult body.

So, where is God? Where was He when I entered the deepest, darkest, steepest valley of my life with nothing left but desperation and hopelessness? Where was He when He began to chisel away at my armor of defenses? Where was He when with each blow of His hammer, I felt the chisel as it gradually forced its way further and further through my armor? Where was He when I cried out in agony from the pain of my depression and anxiety? Where was He when I cried out saying, "I can't take this anymore," and all I heard was silence except for the thumping of my desperate heart? Lack of answers to my desperate questions is not evidence that God is not loving or not present.

I discovered that He is right where He has always been and always will be; right there in the midst of the blood, the guts, and the whole gory mess. I believe this because Jesus promised "Lo I am with you always to the close of the age" (Matthew 28:20) and "Encourages us to hold fast to the confession of our hope without wavering" (Hebrews 10:23). I feel His nearness when Jesus says "I will pray the Father, and He will give you another Counselor, to be with you forever, even the Spirit of truth;... you know him, for he dwells with you, and will be in you. I will not leave you desolate; I will come to you" (John 14:16-18). I experienced that God is faithful as He promised and I gradually started to get better emotionally.

So, with a God who is faithful will not leave us, encourages us, and is always with us; why doesn't He intervene, rescue us, and keep us from hurting? He could! But sometimes He doesn't. I am learning to trust in Jesus and His promises that are beyond my understanding and belief. I extend the arm of faith to trust God in spite of my feelings and past experiences. I think that when I don't hear that "still small voice" it may be because God does not see that I am mature enough to hear or comprehend what He might say during those deep dark moments; or there may be a hindrance to hope that I need to confess as sin.

In using Holy Scriptures to support my beliefs, I am careful that I keep within the context in which it is written. It is possible, and has been done countless times, to take Scriptures out of context to substantiate any number of topics, platforms, beliefs, and ideologies. The Holy Bible must be studied in its entirety, not in bits and pieces. Just as I study the entire Holy Bible; I must take an entire, deep, deep, honest look at myself; and examine my life according to His Word. Some things I have seen in myself that I need to confess and work through in my relationship with God are; restlessness in waiting upon God, dissatisfaction with what I do have, complaining about how He is doing things, envy over what He is doing for others, trying to manipulate God, frustration when my plans are thwarted, and blaming God for life instead of taking personal responsibility for my actions.

To be rescued there are some things I need to remember. God does not promise that I will not have trials, but He does promise that He will go through my troubles with me. At the same time, Satan is alive and well. He is working overtime in my life to lie and destroy my faith in God. When I am feeling low, I am most vulnerable to Satan's wiles and temptations while he is throwing me curves, fastballs, sliders, and change-ups to keep my batting average as low as possible. At the same time, God who is faithful, is speaking to me in a "still small voice" and telling me to keep my eye on the ball and not on the pitcher's form, windup, or delivery. The enemies of my faith, as identified in the Catechism (Grimsby, 1941), are the devil, the world, and my own flesh. God is greater than any one of these and able to help me be victorious in prayer to the Father through His only begotten Son Jesus, and by the power of the Holy Spirit to conquer all of them and set me free.

**See Appendix for Red Flags Indicate that Immediate Help is Needed**

# Chapter 50
## Hurting From Clinical Depression, the Joy of Relief, Forgiveness, Freedom in God

Clinical Depression is a condition of feeling melancholy that is characterized by excessive anger, sadness, anxiety, negative thoughts, suicidal tendencies, feelings of helplessness, uselessness, lack of purpose and a thin sense of meaning in life. It can cause changes in bodily function, sleeping, eating and other disorders. Feelings are a mirror of the way one is thinking; and emotions follow thoughts.

One way that I deal with depression in my life is through a relationship with God's Holy Spirit. Faith empowers me to believe that I am a child of God, an heir of the Lord on High, baptized into Christ, risen with Christ and nothing can separate me from God. Joy is in the "knowing that in everything God works for good with those who love Him, who are called according to his purpose" (Romans 8:28).... With further encouragement to our faith that "in all these things we are more than conquerors through him who loved us. For I am sure that neither death, nor life, nor angels, nor principalities, nor things present, nor things to come, nor powers, nor height, nor depth, nor anything else in all creation, will be able to separate us from the love of God in Christ Jesus our Lord" (Romans 8:37-38).

Pain from emotional events are real at the moment and sometimes I forget or ignore the joy of relief when the pain subsides. Like hitting my thumb accidentally with a hammer, I feel the joy of relief when the physical pain is no longer there. When I choose God's love and promises to acknowledge joy and healing in my life, God enables me not only to experience that joy of relief, but to be able to use it as a Divine Force in my bag of tools to use when life or Satan throws me one of those curve balls I am not expecting, or a dart that I feel is so un-God-like, so unfair as I travel through life. As a believer, I have the Holy Spirit dwelling in me to be that Divine Force to make changes in my responses to emotional pain and hurts from others.

How does casting my emotional baggage on God work for me? I have discovered that emotional and spiritual healing works best if I humble myself before Christ. When I recognize that God alone is God and I am not God, I put myself in a humble position to truly receive God's healing grace for my pain. By humbling myself, listening to God and combining God's Holy Word with prayer I find wisdom, discernment and a building up of my personal faith that gives me the assurance of joy, insight and relief. Daily reading God's Word, meditating on that Word, and prayer working together are a must for those seeking healing. Being in the Word helps me relate warmly to God and promotes spiritual growth through developing good attitudes while I read and receive what God is saying to me. Prayer is my connection to God for two-way communication.

### How do valleys of despair become freedom from emotional pain?

Recently I was betrayed by a longtime friend and deer hunting buddy informing me that I could no longer hunt on the land he manages, and I was very angry. It became clear to me that at first I was ungodly, unkind and rude in my response to him, but eventually was more godly than I could have shown before. At first, I have to admit, I was deeply hurt and definitely angry. After thinking through the situation, offering a prayer for wisdom, and guidance, and listening for that "still small voice," while remembering the scripture of not letting the sun go down on my anger; a realization came to me which would ultimately help me decide what I was going to do as a result of all this mess of being inconsiderate, very angry, hostile, losing my place to hunt, miscommunication, false charges, distrust, unfair accusations, and many other descriptive adjectives that could accurately describe the mean spirited betrayal that had taken place. By the Holy Spirit I was able to admit to myself that I did have at least a small part in the problem and not enough in the solution. I acknowledged to God my part of the responsibility for our falling out, and prayed to be sensitive to consequences for my behaviors that may have caused my friend any difficulty. It is true that when I was angry at the betrayal, I actually did have the right to be angry because we had a firm agreement, but that did not give me the right to be revengeful and vindictive; and it made the necessity of forgiving my buddy even more clear.

Where did that friend's betrayal take me? It actually took me through yet another valley. The designated place mutually agreed upon for us to hunt there meant that much to me. Denying me access was a really big deal because hunting is one of my favorite activities that inspires me and I had worked out the best arrangements with friends that I could ever have. While in this valley I experienced a grievous feeling of no longer being a friend, of being betrayed, of losing my place and abandoned as part of a deer hunting group that I'd been in for years, and it hurt me deeply that my friend of longstanding would betray me by eliminating my right to hunt on that place where I had hunted for years. God gave me the strength to forgive; I forgave my buddy and the pain of this enormous loss subsided when I asked God to heal that emotional wound. I experienced the joy of being free and the joy of being able to explore countless new venues. I discovered that the challenges encountered actually opened up new opportunities.

After losing my spot with the deer hunting group I checked with the County Conservation Officer and discovered that my hunting days are not over. Positive doors for hunting opened up so that I can hunt on county land which happens to be adjacent to the land I had been hunting on. One neighbor also invited me to hunt and trap on her land. I learned that when I experience a valley that God is there to help me and that by taking personal responsibility for my actions and forgiving I am free.

# Chapter 51
## Faith for the Journey of life Gives Hope to My Depressed Brain

How does faith interact with deep dark valleys, emotional pain, unhealed wounds and depression? In order to survive such emotional and psychological episodes in life it takes faith, courage, perseverance, determination and a purpose. It requires a plan with spiritual practices that help us to abide in Christ.

One cannot be spiritually healthy without being emotionally healthy; nor emotionally healthy without being spiritually healthy. The pathway for spiritual health is knowing yourself that you may know God. To be spiritually healthy requires a commitment "to order one's entire life in such a way that the love of Christ comes before all else" (Scazzero, p. 195). It is consciously keeping God at the center of our lives, to have a desire to be with God and to love him above all else. This means to me that I must have faith for life that requires an intentional spiritual growth plan combined with God's Word.

For those of us who have or are experiencing a clinical depression, anxiety, or bipolar condition, or having a series of rough times and cruddy days, I give you the gift of Max Lucado's Survivor's Creed (Lucado, 2013).

"You'll get through this. It won't be painless. It won't be quick.
But God will use this mess for good. In the meantime, don't be foolish or naïve.
But don't despair either. With God's help, you will get through this."

Yes with God's help, I will get through this. I use Max's creed almost on a daily basis to help me get through the day.

God has placed us in physical bodies as a "vessel" for what is on the inside. Unfortunately, thanks to Adam and Eve and Satan's nasty tricks, our world is fallen and besieged by disease, sickness, hatred, wars, and everything unGod-like. As a result our "vessels" can have cracks, breakage, and rugged appearance. Regardless of how the vessel looks or what it seems like, I/we have the guarantee that God looks at the contents; what is inside and not the outward appearance. I have exchanged my sinful heart for Christ's Righteousness that makes me a believer. God looks at me through the special glasses of His Righteousness that filters out everything unChristlike from his heavenly perspective!

G = God's
R = Riches
A = At
C = Christ's
E = Expense

Another analogy that I like is to compare the brain to a finely tuned V-8 engine like one in a car that will run the quarter mile in 8 seconds or less. If the engine in my car runs right it performs well. When my brain is healthy and functional, I experience peace and confidence in God's sustaining grace each day regardless of temptations, Satan's arrows, disappointments, fears or valleys because with God's help I can get through whatever comes to me in life. I am responsible for my responses to the happenings in my life. God is with me every day; dwelling inside me. When I dwell in God's love I also dwell in God (1 John 4). He has given that promise to all of us. For hope, help, and trust in God's promises, I must get my strength from His Word.

Sure, our background and circumstances may have influenced our thoughts or who we became; but I am responsible for the person I become and my responses to the happenings in my life.

# Chapter 52
## Trials Seen through His Presence Gives Encouragement on the Journey of Life

I think there is a misconception that once a person becomes a Christian, they no longer experience trials and tribulations, or if they do, they are few and far between. Another myth is that when a person like myself does experience the deep dark valleys it's because of the lack of faith. Not true! Just because I am a child of God does not mean that I am any more immune to trials, tribulations, or despair than anyone else. God certainly allowed Job to be tested. Job experienced tremendous trials, tribulations, loss, and deep dark valleys.

I discovered that if I choose to carry my own burdens God would let me; but God is near when I want to be forgiven and give Him my burdens. He is more than willing to deliver me and take my burdens to the Cross. Because God's yoke is easy and His burden is light I can tell whose yoke it is I'm carrying by asking; is it heavy or is it light? God will heal us from any ingrained hurt; but we have to be willing to allow Him to do that. God gives me a new song and a happy heart and "he knows the way that I take; when he has first tried me I shall come forth as gold" (Job 23:10 ).

Several years ago I was presented with the opportunity to be a board member of a faith based fledgling group to provide needed services to the elderly, disabled, and handicapped individuals in our county. Thinking that much of my past, education, on-the-job training, and grant writing experience would contribute to the cause I agreed to be a member of the new governing board. What I soon learned was that the other board members ministered to me more than I blessed them! Sometimes God's call comes through His "still small voice" and I realized that He is guiding me to His Purpose for my life through Jesus Christ.

I know that all of this may sound like I have gone "Spiritually Overboard." But when someone is overboard it takes a lifeline to save the person. When someone who has had so much grief heaped on his plate like me, sometimes a lifeline is all that is left for the person to grasp onto regardless of good intentions or well-wishes from family and friends. I know of no other life-line that has a 100% success rate on the part of the life-line thrower.

Fortunately at some point I began to recognize how God was working in my life to set me free. It happened none too soon. I finally realized that God might have other plans for me. It has taken over 70 years, 3 near death experiences, 3 psych ward hospitalizations, forgiving others and being forgiven, many prayers, and daily reading the Bible for me to finally be comfortable with where I am now physically, mentally, emotionally, as well as spiritually. When I chose to acknowledge and accept God's presence, listen and be obedient to His Holy Word and His "still small voice," there can be no other result than to be set free. I believed His promise that He would be my "Abba" Father.

# Chapter 53
## Therapy That Has Worked Freedom for Me

If brain chemistry gets out-of-whack it can wreak havoc with our moods, behaviors and bodily functions. When this happens medications may be necessary. That is why a psychiatrist is so important in dealing with such conditions. A counselor or therapist is equally important and should always play a role in the treatment of the whole person and the two must work together as a team.

In addition to medicinal therapy prescribed by a psychiatrist there are numerous forms of therapy in use today. There are group therapy sessions, class instruction, one-on-one talk sessions, self-talk, desensitization, journaling feelings and thoughts, and a combination that can work together for one's wellbeing. I feel this is extremely important from personal experience; a Christian psychiatrist and a Christian therapist should be mandatory because Christianity brings a necessary dimension to the process of healing.

One of the therapies that seems to have been effective for me is Cognitive Behavioral Therapy which is a type of psychotherapeutic treatment that helps patients understand their thoughts and feelings and how these thoughts and feelings might influence their behaviors. The underlying concept of CBT is that our thoughts and feelings play a fundamental role in our behavior. The purpose of CBT is to teach us that while we cannot control every aspect of the world around us, we can take control of how we interpret and deal with things in our environment. Cognitive Behavioral Therapy(CBT) is commonly used to treat a wide range of disorders including phobias, addictions, depression and anxiety. CBT is generally short-term and focused on helping clients deal with a very specific problem. During my course of treatment I learned how to identify and change destructive or disturbing thought patterns that have had a negative influence on my behavior over a long period of time. Even though Cognitive Behavioral Therapy has been very beneficial for me it has also been extremely difficult for me to do. During the process of CBT I learned that I am a person of extreme "black or white" thinking. This blocked my ability to express my feelings especially when dealing with trauma and other issues of my past. My thinking was so rigid that everything was either right or wrong, left or right, black or white with no in-between. Like Roy Wisner's comment "some minds are like concrete - thoroughly mixed up but permanently set." Black or white thinking leaves no room for any middle ground, extenuating circumstances or for other thought processes; and often times no room for God. Being so rigid, especially as a youngster, led to many unfair confrontations and resulting consequences on my part. The CBT forced me to think outside my box and led me to begin thinking in different ways about myself and my personal issues. This allowed me to begin thinking in more abstract terms which began to break down my walls of being so rigid and judgmental in my thought processes. My therapist would have to frequently remind me to be more curious and not so judgmental. CBT opened up a whole new window of useful, constructive, non-rigid, non-judgmental ways of looking at myself together with my issues; and to make more room for God as well as others. What a feeling of relief, healing and being set free!

Another form of psychotherapy that has become quite popular is Acceptance and Commitment Therapy(ACT). To define Acceptance and Commitment Therapy I refer to Steven C. Hayes, PhD, the originator of ACT. He says, "It is an empirically supported approach that takes a new and unexpected way in dealing with the issues of happiness and life satisfaction. Instead of teaching new techniques to pursue happiness, ACT teaches ways to undermine struggle, avoidance, and loss of the moment." CBT and ACT are the other therapeutic approaches used during my care. These are the ones I remember the most.

## GRIEFSHARE

Probably the most useful approach for me is the one I am currently involved in; GriefShare is an intuitive and interactive program that is Bible based and deals with the results of death of loved ones, pain of loss, associated emotions, feelings, and how to move forward. The past should be a rudder to steer you, not an anchor to keep you from moving forward.

Participants are given a workbook, and watch a DVD showing various individuals explaining their respective circumstances, their feelings, emotions, and how they worked through them to move forward to a more healthy way of life, or a new normal. In addition to the DVD, GriefShare consists of a series of thirteen sessions, usually one session per week. During those sessions participants meet with the other individuals in the group to share and understand their feelings as they pertain to their grieving process.

Each session begins with prayer followed by viewing the DVD which features interviews with individuals who are, or were, grieving the loss of loved ones. The video also features interviews with Christian experts concerning various ways to help those during their grieving process.

Following are the topics of each session.
Session 1: Is This Normal?
    Common Responses to the Death of a Loved One

Session 2: Challenges of Grief

Session 3: The Journey of Grief – Part One
    Writing a Grief Letter

Session 4: The Journey of Grief – Part Two
    How to Ask For and Accept Help

Session 5: Grief and Your Relationships
    Caring For Grieving Children
    Being Honest With Your Comforters

Session 6: Why?

Session 7: Guilt and Anger
   Why Should I Forgive?

Session 8: Complicating Factors
   Post – traumatic Stress Disorder

Session 9: Stuck

Session 10: Lessons of Grief – Part One
   Coping With Grief During Holidays

Session 11: Lessons of Grief – Part Two

Session 12: Heaven
   God's Forgiveness: An Unlikely Source of Joy and Comfort

Session 13: What Do I Live For Now?
   Will Life Return To Normal?
   A New Normal

The video is followed by a small group discussion that encourages participants to talk about how the video and the workbook relates to their life and grieving process. Each session is closed with prayer.

Presently I have attended the thirteen GriefShare sessions for three years and I plan to attend again when the program resumes. I found that the second time proved to be more beneficial than the first; the third more beneficial than the second, and I assume future sessions will be even more beneficial.

What I personally found helpful was that I could relate to portions of the video as well as the following discussions. It was as if some of the individuals speaking in the video were speaking directly to me. The support from other participants coheres with the topic and is particularly helpful.

The facilitators of our group were John and Bonnie who have both experienced loss and tragedy in their lives and have been facilitating this group of GriefShare for a number of years. A member of my group, Annette K., shares that "GriefShare is an explosive Christian based program to help those grieving. Individuals in the group are thoughtful, kind, courteous, but above all loving. I feel very safe in this environment. Our moderators have traveled the grief road so their input is invaluable. Everyone grieves at a different level. Through GriefShare I am coming to grips with my loss little by little." Jolene shares her experience in my group. "GriefShare has helped me to feel I can move on and expect, with God's help, to even enjoy happiness and fulfillment in my future. I especially liked being part of a group where I felt comfortable with sharing our stories."

I hope this endeavor has helped place and develop a meaning and purpose in your lives according to God's Word and the work of the Holy Spirit. God loves you deeply and cares for you regardless of your circumstances. Trust in Jesus!

© MMXIV GriefShare, a ministry of Church Initiative. Visit GriefShare.org to find a group near you.

# APPENDIX

**Red Flags Indicate that I Need Immediate Help**

Following are areas of concern that are red-flags indicating that immediate help is needed.

This may not be an exhaustive list but these are ones I am familiar with because I have personally experienced each and every one of them during my life. Sometimes more than one occur simultaneously. I am writing these in my own words.

**Thoughts of injuring yourself**

If you are, or have been, having thoughts or feelings of injuring yourself or others you need to seek professional help immediately and I mean right now. If you are unable or feel you cannot make that decision, please allow others to make that decision for you. It is that important.

Believe me I know, I've been there. Fortunately when my decision making processes became clouded I had and I continue to have, a loving, caring, and supportive family that was courageous enough to step in and make that necessary decision. Had it not been for them we would not be having this discussion.

**Confusion**

If you suddenly find yourself confused and have difficulty understanding what should have previously been easily understood, that could potentially be another red flag. Even though you may have had excellent problem solving skills you suddenly find yourself confused and don't understand why.

## E.D.

This can be one of those areas easily dismissed or swept under the rug so-to-speak and not given much validity because of so many other variables that could come into play. Even though there are a plethora of reasons for erectile dysfunction in men it should always be considered a red flag associated with mental or emotional pain. Because of its sensitive nature to men it is often never discussed.

## Grief

It is a given that we all have or will experience grief at some point in our lives. It is the natural result of living and cannot be avoided. When the stumbling block of sorrow from the past and the guilt of it surfaces and keeps on ruminating, or immobilizes you from moving forward that should be considered another red flag. Moving on and moving forward are not the same thing. Moving on suggests you are leaving something or someone behind; whereas moving forward suggests continuing forward after acknowledging the past.

## Voices

Voices? This phenomenon can be controversial and easily dismissed. Sometimes when a person is in a deep emotional valley; an actual voice may be heard. A person may hear their own name with no one present, or another person's name; or sometimes a single word, a short phrase, or even a brief sentence. This is a red flag.

## Irritability

Another red flag should be when a person becomes easily irritated. At the time you become quickly defensive, or short with others when completely unwarranted, irritability can be a problem and potentially serious. Watch out for being defensive for no apparent reason. Sometimes it's alright to be angry because you have a right to be angry without seeking revenge.

## Low Energy

This is also one of those areas where there can be a multitude of reasons or causes for low energy. If after all reasons for low energy have been explored and exhausted and it still feels like you are running on fumes; it is likely related to your mood or emotions. If you find yourself frequently falling asleep during the day even though you had a restful night's sleep, or you don't like driving any distance for fear of falling asleep at the wheel should be considered a red flag.

## Mystery Aches and Pains

When one experiences body aches and pains in various parts of the body for no apparent reason when all possible causes and conditions have been explored and eliminated this should be a concern. Moods and emotions can play weird things with our bodies and when they occur it should be considered a red flag.

## Recklessness

When your mood or emotions have been assaulted and unfairly impacted your senses can become numb or altered. As a result, you can become reckless and careless which is considered to be a red flag.

## Concentration

If you are having a lot of trouble staying with one thought, idea, task, or job to completion; you are probably experiencing a symptom of poor concentration. Given, there are numerous reasons for poor concentration. But, with all the obvious ones eliminated this should also be considered a red flag.

## Short-term Memory

Trying to remember something that should be, or would ordinarily be readily retrievable, and yet resulting in one of those embarrassing distinct blanks can be extremely frustrating. There are countless reasons for not being able to remember. When despite all other issues this seems to become a stand-alone-issue it should also be considered a red flag.

## Frustration

Who has not been frustrated at some time or another when things do not seem to go as planned. We all have had some degree of frustration as part of life. With everything considered, when frustration seems to be running at warp speed, it is time to stop and make an assessment of your mood and emotions since this could be another red flag.

## Indecisiveness

All of us may experience a time when we have difficulty making a decision. When a person becomes emotionally paralyzed to the point of being unable to make a decision, it becomes an important symptom. Personally, I really like things to be neat and tidy with everything in its respective place. Unfortunately, I cannot organize my way out of a wet paper bag with a hole in it! If someone was to take a tour of my basement they would immediately say, " David you are a hoarder. You don't have a filing system you have a piling system!" For the life of me, for reasons unknown to me, I am unable to decide what goes where, when, or why. For me this is a red-flag issue.

Red Flags are important for me to keep in mind because these red flags can and do affect my mood and emotions to the degree that professional intervention is warranted and necessary. There may be others that are just as important. As long as I continue with the plan of intervention that has been laid out for me I am doing fine. I see my psychiatrist on a regular basis which is about every three months, or sooner if indicated. We discuss my mood, my emotions and my medications. I also see a therapist about once per month. It has taken years, but I have finally been blessed with a fantastic psychiatrist and therapists. That has not always been the case. Over the years I have seen four or five psychiatrists and countless therapists or counselors. Things are going well with the team I am working with

166

now. It seems that finding the right fit with professionals is sometimes like finding the right mechanic for your car, the right suit that fits, or the right person to help you manage your finances.

Finally, I must reiterate with all the emphasis I can muster, professional intervention is a must if one is ever going to escape those deep, dark, foreboding valleys of depression, anxiety, and desperation that can lead to a conundrum of mental as well as physical health issues.

# REFERENCES

Arthur, Kay, Precepts for Life, Crosswalk, Online Bible-Based Ministry, 2017.

Barrier, Roger. Crosswalk, Online Bible-Based Ministry; What I want to Tell the Person Having Suicidal Thoughts, 2017.

Holy Bible, Revised Standard Version (RSV), Translated from the original tongues set forth and revised 1901 and compared with the most ancient authorities and revised A.D. 1952, A.J. Holman Company, Philadelphia.

Dobson, James, When God Doesn't Make Sense, Tyndale House Publishing Inc., Wheaton, IL, 1993.

Finke, Greg, Joining Jesus on His Mission, Tenth Power Publishing, Elgin, IL, 2014.

GriefShare, a ministry of Church Initiative.Visit GriefShare.org to find a group near you.

Harris, Russ, The Happiness Trap: How to Stop Struggling and Start Living, Trumpeter, Boulder, 2008.

Hayes, S.C, Strosahl, K.D., & Wilson, K.G. (2012). Acceptance and commitment therapy: The process and practice of mindful change (2nd edition). New York, NY: The Guilford Press.

Henry Grimsby, An Explanation of the Catechism, Augsburg Publishing House, 1941.

Hontz, Marilyn, Listening for God. Tyndale House Publishers, Inc., Wheaton, IL, 2004.

Jeremiah, David, What in the World is Going On, Turning Point Ministries, San Diego, CA, 2008.

Jordan, Rebecca, Prayers for Healing, Crosswalk: Online Bible-Based Ministry, 2013.

Lucado, Max, You'll Get Through This, Thomas Nelson, Nashville, TN, 2013.

McMenamin, Cindi, 7 Ways to Ask for the Love You Need. Crosswalk, Online Bible-based Ministry, 2017.

Rivers, Francine, 5 Ways the Demons from Our Past are Controlling Us. Crosswalk: Online Bible-Based Ministry, 2018.

Scazzero, Peter: Emotionally Healthy Spirituality, Thomas Nelson, Nashville TN: 2006.

Yancy, Phillip, Where Is God When It Hurts. Zondervan Publishing House, Grand Rapids, MI., 1990.

Young, William, The Shack. Windblown Media, Los Angeles, CA., 2007.